To

J.C.G.

Other books by Doris Wilcox Gilbert

POWER AND SPEED IN READING

BREAKING THE READING BARRIER

STUDY IN DEPTH

THE TURNING POINT IN READING

Breaking

WORD

Englewood Cliffs, New Jersey

the BARRIER

DORIS WILCOX GILBERT

PRENTICE-HALL, INC.

ISBN 0-13-081661-2

Library of Congress Catalog Card No.: 77-173596

10   9   8   7   6   5

Photo credits: p. 1, Goodyear-Canada; p. 19, International Typographic
Composition Association, Larry Kline, and AIGA; p. 50, Hillsborough Community
College, Career Brochures, Tampa, Florida; p. 64, Standard Oil Company
(New Jersey); p. 109, Raymond Juschkus, The Chase Manhattan Bank; p. 136,
United Nations; p. 150, Eastern Airlines.

PRENTICE-HALL INTERNATIONAL, INC., *London*
PRENTICE-HALL OF AUSTRALIA, PTY. LTD., *Sydney*
PRENTICE-HALL OF CANADA, LTD., *Toronto*
PRENTICE-HALL OF INDIA PRIVATE LTD., *New Delhi*
PRENTICE-HALL OF JAPAN, INC., *Tokyo*

Contents

Section Two

Section Three

Section Four

Section Five

Section Six

Section Seven

Section Eight

Section Nine

Section Ten

Section Eleven

Section Twelve

Keys,   *184*

Preface

It is the purpose of this book to extend and enrich vocabulary and build spelling competence: thus it should contribute to precise and effective communication. In general it is intended for use in occupational courses in community and junior colleges, extension and adult education centers, in business schools, and in training programs of business and industry.

It is not written for people with a flair for words and high percentile standings on college level tests of verbal competence, or for those who are virtual strangers to the language. Rather, it is for people who have made a good start with words and their usage, but recognize the need to improve if they are to increase their vocational effectiveness, raise their course grades, and play effective roles as citizens and individuals in the world of today.

In any educational program and in almost any career, word competence is essential. Our modern society is dominated by directives and instructions, by news reports and editorials, by lectures, and by countless sources of information and pleasure—all of them word-based. People who can not communicate, even the highly intelligent, are sharply limited in the goals they can hope to achieve. They are blocked, as it were, by a barrier. It is the purpose of this book to help break that barrier.

The approach is eclectic. It uses a number of methods, not one alone.

Where organized instruction is not available, the work can be done independently. Discussions and explanations are a part of each section, and directions are provided for all exercises and drills. Answers are provided in the Appendix.

But communication through words goes beyond reading and writing to include listening and speaking, and much is to be gained, therefore, from well-structured class discussions and from the stimulation of an instructor who knows and enjoys words, passes judgment on colloquial usage and slang, and tailors special drills to the needs of the group or of individuals. Special classes are not essential. There is excellent reason to include word study in reading improvement classes, in speech or writing sections, or in other English courses.

A Note to the Instructor

MEASUREMENT OF WORD COMPETENCE

When research findings established conclusively the close relationship between word competence and effectiveness in the language arts, questions were asked about norms and specific objectives, and in recent decades there have been numerous attempts to determine the size of the vocabulary for each of the academic levels. But there has been a great diversity in the findings. Scholars have not been in complete agreement as to what constitutes "knowledge" of a word. Furthermore, they have used a variety of techniques of investigation.

There have been four important methods: counting the different words occurring in the spontaneous conversation of an individual, counting the different words appearing in his written work, noting the responses to stimulus words, and estimating the size of the total vocabulary from correct responses to selected lists of words. When the method has involved reactions to set lists, it has been established that vocabulary estimates based on samplings from an unabridged dictionary are much larger than those based on samplings from an abridged dictionary.[1]

A count of the number of words in an individual's vocabulary, no matter what technique is used, is time-consuming and usually not justified. As a rule, it is better to begin determination of competence in terms of norms from standardized tests. When time and the budget permit, it is helpful to precede class instruction or individual work with the administration of one or more of these tests. Equivalent forms can be administered midway and at the end of the program to measure, in part, the gains.

For the names of standardized tests suitable for students with whom you are working, consult the *Fifth Mental Measurements Yearbook*[2]. Very often tests of word competence are included in batteries of reading tests. The *Yearbook* provides statements on validity and reliability.

An informal test of word competence is included in Section One of this manual. It is made up of words featured later in the lists, drills, and exercises. Scores from the subtests and answers to the questions in the Personal Inventory should provide diagnostic information about the knowledge and approaches of the individual at the start of the program. The test is repeated in Section Twelve and a second Inventory is provided. The findings, after a reasonable period of intensive work, should make possible a partial appraisal of gains.

MATERIALS OF THE MANUAL

The materials of the manual are designed to extend vocabulary, sharpen the knowledge and usage of words already partly familiar, and build spelling competence. They are also

[1] Nancy Larrick, "How Many Words Does a Child Know?" *The Reading Teacher*, December, 1954, pp. 100–104.

[2] Oscar K. Buros, *Fifth Mental Measurements Yearbook* (Highland Park, N.J.: The Gryphon Press, 1965).

intended to contribute to the establishment of skills and approaches basic to viability. In this day of rapid scientific advances, jobs and job requirements are subject to frequent change. For any individual a vocabulary suitable for the needs of today may be totally insufficient for those of tomorrow.

Effectiveness involves not merely possession of a broad knowledge of useful words in isolation, but a sensitivity to specialized uses of words in context. It requires word sense, word consciousness, and independence in attacking new words. Especially, it demands word interest.

WORD LISTS

Words selected for Lists One through Twelve are of two main types. First there are terms from a number of occupational areas of key importance today—from the Health Services, Government Work, Building Trades, Driver Occupations, and Aviation, for example. Most were selected from the *Occupational Outlook Handbook*,[3] and include such terms as *antidote, concussion, routeman, journeyman, actuary,* and *underwriter.* While they come from special career fields, a knowledge of their meanings is essential to the understanding of topics in today's news. No odd words are included and no highly technical words needed only by the specialist. All the words in the lists should be a part of the general background of today.

Second, there are the general words belonging to no special field. These are words like *authentic, maneuver, viable, potent, adversary, versatile, paradox,* and *salient.* Most were selected from news magazines, then checked with the core vocabulary of the Educational Developmental Laboratories.[4]

EXERCISES, DRILLS, WORK SUGGESTIONS

The exercises and drills—of several types—are usually accompanied by explanations and suggestions. Some are designed to build competence in arriving independently at the meanings of strange words by directing attention to the roles of word parts and of context.

Others point to the importance of singling out words to be added to the active vocabulary and using systematic techniques for mastery. Both meanings and spellings are considered. For the words of the manual lists, the exercises provide a wide variety of opportunities for checking progress.

Finally, since a major objective is the sharpening and refining of word knowledge and usage, many of the drills are planned directly toward that end. Some call for judgment of different definitions of a familiar word, or for formulation of definitions that are at once adequate and concise. Others require the listing of sharply different meanings for the same word, or for the selection or proposal of words suitable in particular situations.

Some of the words in these materials are the contributions of students who found that they presented difficulties because of popular misconceptions about their meanings or confusion with other similar words. *Biennial* is often confused with *biannual,* for example, and *ominous* with *omnibus.*

[3] United States Department of Labor, *Occupational Outlook Handbook,* Bulletin 1450 (Washington, D.C.: Superintendent of Documents, U.S. Government Printing Office, 1967).

[4] Stanford Taylor and Helen Frankenpohl, *A Core Vocabulary* (New York: Educational Developmental Laboratories, 1960).

Included in some of the exercises are directives like *compare, contrast, summarize, trace,* and *evaluate.* A clear grasp of the meanings of these words is prerequisite to competence in answering essay examination questions.

Drills and exercises are of several types:

a) Fill-in sentences
b) Matching exercises
c) Multiple choice items
d) Analogy fill-ins
e) True-false statements
f) Flexibility of usage items

PROCEDURE

The procedure is flexible and instruction can be adapted to groups or individuals of widely different interests and aims. In a "closed" class, tailored to the needs of a particular occupational group, supplemental materials can be worked out using the technical terms and words peculiar to that field. Take, for example, a class of employees in an electric power plant. The instructor can study in advance the materials with which these people have to work, and develop drills like those in the manual, but using such terms as *ampere, ohm, electrode, rheostat, transformer, volt,* and *farad.*

Vocabulary instruction is often offered as part of another course, such as reading improvement. In such a course many of the drills and exercises in the manual can be done independently by the student, and class time can be reserved for timed tests, pronunciation drills, and consideration of problems and words of special importance to the group.

CONFERENCES

No matter what general plan of procedure is used, office conferences at frequent intervals are invaluable in clarifying problems, formulating recommendations tailored to the needs of the student, and checking progress.

A manilla folder for each conferee simplifies the task of keeping together test records and conference notes. As the program progresses, the record becomes cumulative and points to the nature of the improvement. Conferences at the end of a reasonable period of intensive work can be used to summarize key gains and offer suggestions for the future.

SELECTED REFERENCES

Dictionaries

American Heritage Dictionary of the English Language. New York: American Heritage Publishing Co., Inc., 1969.

Fowler, H. W., *A Dictionary of Modern English Usage.* New York and London: Oxford University Press, 1965.

Fowler, H. W., and F. G. Fowler, *The Concise Oxford Dictionary of Current English.* rev. ed. New York: Oxford University Press, 1964.

Hamburger, Edward, *A Business Dictionary*. Englewood Cliffs, N.J.: Prentice-Hall, Inc., 1967.

Lewis, Norman, ed., *The New Roget's Thesaurus in Dictionary Form*, rev. ed. Garden City, N.Y.: Garden City Books, 1961.

Murray, J. H., H. Bradley, W. A. Craigie, and C. T. Onions, *The Oxford English Dictionary*. New York: Oxford University Press, 1933.

Picturesque Word Origins. Springfield, Mass.: G. and C. Merriam Company, 1933.

The Random House Dictionary of the English Language. New York: Random House, Inc., 1969.

Roget's *Thesaurus*. New York: Thomas Y. Crowell Company, 1962.

Thorndike, E. I., and C. L. Barnhart, *Comprehensive Desk Dictionary*. Palo Alto, Calif.: Scott, Foresman & Company, 1962.

Webster's *New World Dictionary of the American Language*, 2nd College Ed. Cleveland and New York: World Publishing Company, 1970.

Webster's *New Third International Dictionary*. Springfield, Mass.: G. and C. Merriam Company, 1966.

Webster's *Seventh New Collegiate Dictionary*. Springfield, Mass.: G. and C. Merriam Company, 1967.

Books About Words

Bodmer, Frederick, *The Loom of Language*. New York: W. W. Norton & Company, Inc., 1944.

Dale, Edgar, and Taher Razik, *Bibliography of Vocabulary Studies*. Columbus, Ohio: The Ohio State University Press, 1963.

Deighton, Lee C., *Vocabulary Development in the Classroom*. New York: Columbia University Press, 1959.

Dow, Gwyneth, *Uncommon Common Sense*. Melbourne, Australia: F. W. Cheshire Property, 1962.

O'Connor, Johnson, *Vocabulary and Success*. Hoboken, N.J.: Human Engineering Laboratories, Stevens Institute of Technology, 1934.

Petty, Walter, Curtis Herold, and Earline Stoll, *The State of Knowledge about the Teaching of Vocabulary*. Champaign, Ill.: National Council of Teachers of English, 1968.

Potter, Simeon, *Our Language*. Baltimore: Penguin, 1950.

Taylor, Stanford E., Helen Franckenpohl, Arthur McDonald, and Nancy Joline, *Word Clues*. Huntington, N.Y.: Educational Developmental Laboratories, 1960.

Vocabulary Builders

Brown, James L., *Programmed Vocabulary*. New York: Appleton-Century-Crofts, 1964.

Curry, Robert L., and Toby Rigby, *Reading Independence Through Word Analysis*. Norman, Okla.: University Book Exchange, University of Oklahoma, 1967.

Davis, Nancy, *Vocabulary Improvement*. New York: McGraw-Hill Book Company, 1967.

De Vitis, A. A., and R. J. Warner, *Words in Context*. New York: Appleton-Century-Crofts, 1961.

Funk, Wilfred, and Norman Lewis, *30 Days to a More Powerful Vocabulary*. New York: Funk & Wagnalls Company, Inc., 1949.

Gilmartin, John, *Increase Your Vocabulary*, 2nd ed. Englewood Cliffs, N.J.: Prentice-Hall, Inc., 1957.

Goodman, Roger B., and David Lewin, *New Ways to Greater Word Power*. New York: Dell Publishing Company, Inc., 1955.

Hardwick, H. C., *Words Are Important*. New York: Hammond Publishing Company, 1964.

Hart, Archibald, *Twelve Ways to Build a Vocabulary*. New York: E. P. Dutton & Co., Inc., 1945.

Lee, Donald, *Harbrace Vocabulary Guide*. New York: Harcourt Brace Jovanovich, 1956.

Levine, Harold, *Vocabulary for the College Bound Student*. New York: AMSCO School Publications, Inc., 1965.

Lewis, Norman, *Word Power Made Easy*. New York: Thomas Y. Crowell Company, 1964.

Monson, S. C., *Word Building*. New York: The Macmillan Company, 1968.

Nurnberg, Maxwell, and Morris Rosenblum, *All About Words*. Englewood Cliffs, N.J.: Prentice-Hall, Inc., 1966.

Books on Spelling

Ayer, Fred, *Gateways to Correct Spelling*, rev. ed. Austin, Texas: The Steck Company, 1960.

Drake, William, *The Way to Spell*. San Francisco, Calif.: Chandler Publishing Company, 1967.

Hook, J. N., *Spelling 1500: A Program*. New York, Harcourt Brace Jovanovich, 1967.

Section One

A NOTE TO THE READER

The physical problems of transmitting messages from place to place have been solved. But as knowledge expands and interests diversify, another problem of communication seems to become more complex—the accurate transmission of ideas from mind to mind. People often have the feeling that they fail to make clear their own meanings, that they fail to grasp precisely the meanings of others.

Today there is a mounting interest in better, more effective communication. One reason is the growing concern, particularly on the part of young adults, with local and world affairs, and the realization that keeping informed is essential. Again, new careers are opening up in business and related occupations, in the health services, in printing and advertising, radio and television, in the agri-business and forestry, in government services, and in other areas. But opportunities are increasing most rapidly for those with suitable education and training, and with the ability to adapt readily to changes in job requirements. Long-term employment and promotion depend to an important extent upon communication competence in matters related to the job.

One of the barriers to effective communication in speech is faulty pronunciation. Another is the failure to specify: "That thing on the desk" may be an atlas or an almanac, a stapler or a stylus, a card file or a slide rule, an ink pad or—a black widow spider. Often the meaning is blurred by repetition of a meaningless phrase like "You know?" or "See?"

There are other barriers. None is more obstructive, however, than a poor command of words.

In one sense, speaking, listening, reading, and writing are separate and distinct processes: each is dependent upon its own constellation of skills, abilities, bits of information, and habits of thinking. In another way, however, they are alike. They all have their bases in words.

The materials of this manual are intended to help you extend and enrich your vocabulary and build your spelling competence. Preliminary tests and an inventory will sample your knowledge and approaches at the start. The materials that follow will include lists of important words, suggestions, and exercises of many types designed to add to your active knowledge and selective use of words. A final test and inventory will help you to assess in part the gains that you have made.

A major objective is the development of a deep interest in words and a continuing alertness to those of significance for you. Word competence must be viable. Your independent work with words should begin without delay.

PRELIMINARY TESTS

Read the directions for each of the subtests in this group. Work rapidly without the aid of a dictionary or other reference.

Part A ◆ VOCATIONS AND INDUSTRIES

DIRECTIONS ◆ Indicate your choice of answers by writing the letter on the blank at the right.

1. A business organization supplying gas and electricity to an area is known as
   a) a public utility   b) a brokerage   c) a trust company   1. A

2. A person learning an art or trade is
   a) a journeyman   b) a technician   c) an apprentice   2. C

3. One who fails to pay on time the money he owes is
   a) a felon   b) a defaulter   c) an absconder   3. A ✗ B

4. The sole owner of a business is the
   a) manager   b) superintendent   c) proprietor   4. C

5. One's occupation, business, or trade is his
   a) vocation   b) avocation   c) heritage   5. A

6. A person given work and pay is an
   a) applicant   b) employee   c) employer   6. C ✗ B

7. A detailed list of stock or articles on hand is
   a) an invoice   b) an inventory   c) a budget   7. B

8. The protection, development, and management of natural resources is known as
   a) silviculture   b) conservation   c) agriculture   8. B

9. A part payment is
   a) an installment   b) a promissory note   c) a debit   9. A

10. Engineers who design and supervise the construction of roads, harbors, airfields, bridges, and sewer systems are, essentially,
    a) ceramic engineers   b) chemical engineers   c) civil engineers   10. C

80%

Go on to Part B.

3

Part B ◆ SPECIALISTS

DIRECTIONS ◆ Indicate your choice of answers by writing the letter on the blank at the right.

1. Driver-salesman
   a) chauffeur   b) routeman   c) statistician

   1. *B*

2. One who takes dictation, usually in shorthand, and transcribes the notes on a typewriter
   a) receptionist   b) typist   c) stenographer

   2. *C*

3. The highest ranking representative sent by one country to another
   a) ambassador   b) consul   c) economist

   3. *A*

4. Person trained in the science of atmosphere and the weather
   a) cardiologist   b) cartographer   c) meteorologist

   4. *C*

5. Physician who specializes in the care of infants and children
   a) pediatrician   b) podiatrist   c) orthodontist

   5. *A*

6. One who figures risks, rates, and premiums for insurance companies
   a) bookkeeper   b) teller   c) actuary

   6. *C*

7. One who provides any of a variety of beauty services, such as manicures, haircuts, hairstyling
   a) cosmetologist   b) geologist   c) teletypist

   7. *A*

8. One who buys and sells (e.g., real estate) for others
   a) clerk   b) mason   c) broker

   8. *C*

9. Specialist trained to plan meals to help people recover or maintain good health
   a) restaurateur   b) nurse's aid   c) dietitian

   9. *C*

10. Airline employee who coordinates flight schedules and operations within a given area
    a) copilot   b) pilot   c) dispatcher

    10. *C*

100%

Part C ◆ NOUNS FROM TOMORROW'S JOBS

1. Body of an airplane
   a) chassis   b) fuselage   c) propeller

   1. *A✗ B*

2. Shelter for housing aircraft
   a) hangar   b) garage   c) runway

   2. *A*

3. Device to stop bleeding by compressing a blood vessel
   a) antidote   b) tourniquet   c) anesthetic

   3. *B*

4. Grant of money, especially one made by the government
   a) subsidy   b) annuity   c) franchise

   4. *A*

5. Device for mixing air with gas to make an explosive mixture, as for an automobile engine
a) exhaust   b) carburetor   c) air conditioner   5. _B_

6. Act of paying out
a) disbursement   b) transcription   c) audition   6. _A_

7. Instrument in an aircraft to measure distance above the earth's surface
a) speedometer   b) ignition   c) altimeter   7. _C_

8. Guarantee or pledge
a) warranty   b) premium   c) option   8. _A_

9. The making of textiles, apparel, aircraft, wood products, machinery, and so on
a) manufacture   b) exportation   c) licensing   9. _A_

10. Something expected to produce a profit or income or both
a) withdrawal   b) premium   c) investment   90%   10. _C_

Part D ◆ WORDS OFTEN CONFUSED

DIRECTIONS ◆ Write out the word of your choice on the blank. Save the short lines at right for scoring, later on.

1. A rule, a fundamental belief, or truth is a *principle*/*principal*.

_____   1. ___

2. Truthfulness is *voracity*/*veracity*. _____   2. ___

3. Paper, envelopes, and other writing materials are known as *stationary*/*stationery*. _____   3. ___

4. To order, direct, or give advice is to *proscribe*/*prescribe*.

_____   4. ___

5. One who takes the lead—in a school, for example, or in a business—is the *principal*/*principle*. _____   5. ___

6. To condemn or prohibit is to *proscribe*/*prescribe*. _____   6. ___

7. To give advice is to *council*/*counsel*. _____   7. ___

8. New scientific knowledge is bound to *effect*/*affect* job requirements.

_____   8. ___

9. The team had its full *compliment*/*complement* of outstanding athletes.

_____   9. ___

10. One who leaves his country to settle in another is an *immigrant*/*emigrant* from his native land. _____   10. ___

90%

5

Part E ◆ GETTING THE MEANING FROM THE CONTEXT

DIRECTIONS ◆ Try to discover the meaning of the *italicized* word as it is used in each passage. Then write the meaning on the blank.

1. Celebrating his one hundredth birthday, a man in Melbourne attributed his *longevity* to his lifelong interest in sports.

   _____longtime_____   1.___

2. Unlike many other officials, he was a man of few words; he was known far and wide for his *reticence*.

   _____Quit_____   2.___

3. No words passed between them. Their facial expressions gave *tacit* approval to the suggestion.

   _____   3.___

4. For this group of workers, the committee was not interested in houses rooted to the ground, like those of the past. It was the plan, rather, to construct *mobile* homes.

   _____   4.___

5. The script for the play is concise and to the point. The author has a *laconic* facility with dialogue.

   _____   5.___

6. It was agreed that neither party should take the lead in reporting the story; the announcements were to be made *simultaneously*.

   _____   6.___

7. Some critics accused the manager of waste and extravagance; others went to the opposite extreme and blamed him for his *parsimony*.

   _____   7.___

8. Impelled by *premonitions* of his death, he talked over his affairs with his lawyer and drew up a will.

   _____   8.___

9. There was no plan and no appointment. The meeting of the two was *fortuitous*.

   _____   9.___

10. The boys were as different as night and day. Mark had a selfish concern only for his own interests. Martin was the *altruist*.

   _____   10.___

11. Today psychologists are asking children to draw pictures of their friends and family members in action. These *kinetic* drawings often make clear the nature of the youngsters' problems.

_____ 11.___

12. The quiet delicacy and good taste of the music is seen by the experts as a retreat from the shockingly *blatant* environment in which it is written.

_____ 12.___

13. For some months he has been trying to get his campaign under way. There has been no public announcement, no aboveboard request for funds. Yet he has gained sufficient backing to build up a *clandestine* operation equipped with radio transmitters and carried on by a thousand recruits.

_____ 13.___

14. If the children in the neighborhood rode their bicycles over his lawn, he grew angry; when their noise disturbed him, he lost his temper and shouted at them. He was known for his *irascible* disposition.

_____ 14.___

15. The play was a *perennial* success. Introduced in the 1920's, it remained on stage several years. Brought back in the 1940's, it flourished, and then, in the 1960's, it demonstrated once again its long lasting appeal.

_____ 15.___

16. The disease, which often afflicts the young, is characterized by an uncontrolled *proliferation* of certain white blood cells, which gradually crowd out the vital red blood cells.

_____ 16.___

17. The expression "widow woman" is *redundant.*

_____ 17.___

18. A truck driver and a true believer in advertising slogans, Jim had no *qualms* when he bought the supposedly overhauled car. But then when he drove away with it, he discovered a flaw: the brakes failed.

_____ 18.___

19. One researcher observed that bleeding is encouraged, not *inhibited,* if the ear lobe is chilled.

_____ 19.___

20. The people worry deeply that hard times may reach them. "Our paychecks are bigger, but we take home less," says the mayor, *articulating* the town's major obsession.

_____ 20.___

Part F ✦ ANALOGIES

DIRECTIONS ✦ In each series note the relationship between the first two words. Then choose the two other words which have most nearly the same relationship. Fill in the blanks with their letters in the *same order of relationship*.

EXAMPLE ✦ cat : kitten : : __e__ : __c__
a) tent   b) brake   c) calf   d) quiz   e) cow

The letters *e* and *c* point to the best choices and indicate the order of relationship. A cat is to a kitten as a cow is to a calf.

1. abrupt : gradual : : _A_ : _C_

   a) mobile   b) adjustable   c) immovable   d) new   e) early   1._____

2. physician : patient : : _e_ : _C_

   a) teacher   b) university   c) client   d) parent   e) lawyer   2._____

3. shortage : surfeit : : _e_ : _A_

   a) excess   b) top   c) dawn   d) total   e) lack   3._____

4. convene : assemble : : _____ : _____

   a) assess   b) prescribe   c) adjourn   d) censure   e) criticize   4._____

5. statue : sculptor : : _C_ : _e_

   a) costume   b) curtain   c) writer   d) painter   e) script   5._____

6. confer : conferee : : _B_ : _c_

   a) recur   b) trainee   c) employee   d) employ   e) recurrences   6._____

7. bizarre : bazaar : : _A_ : _C_

   a) night   b) morning   c) knight   d) day   e) knighthood   7._____

8. predict : future : : _B_ : _A_

   a) present   b) past   c) reminisce   d) foretell   e) forget   8._____

9. heart : cardiac : : _B_ : _E_

   a) spinal   b) pulmonary   c) dental   d) digestion   e) lungs   9._____

10. cattle : herd : : _e_ : _A_

    a) covey   b) swarm   c) drove   d) wolves   e) quail   10._____

11. soprano : female : : _D_ : _C_

    a) infant   b) contralto   c) male   d) tenor   e) bass   11._____

8

12. overt : secret : : _____ : _____
   a) cautious   b) rash   c) clever   d) coy   e) humorous   12.___

13. audible : inaudible : : _____ : _____
   a) gustatory   b) visual   c) credible   d) invisible   e) visible   13.___

14. biennial : biannual : : _____ : _____
   a) 16   b) 12   c) 8   d) 4   e) 18   14.___

15. quell : incite : : _____ : _____
   a) harangue   b) ignite   c) extinguish   d) blame   e) decide   15.___

16. word : dictionary : : _____ : _____
   a) library   b) gymnasium   c) book   d) swimming pool   e) vista   16.___

17. adroit : inept : : _____ : _____
   a) skillful   b) studious   c) ailing   d) disobedient   e) awkward   17.___

18. cow : bovine : : _____ : _____
   a) canine   b) lupine   c) snake   d) equine   e) wolf   18.___

19. tricycle : bicycle : : _____ : _____
   a) four   b) three   c) two   d) one   e) zero   19.___

20. boat : water : : _____ : _____
   a) automobile   b) airplane   c) exhaust   d) fuselage   e) air   20.___

21. principal : principle : : _____ : _____
   a) sign   b) order   c) telephone   d) right   e) write   21.___

22. skeptical : credulous : : _____ : _____
   a) covert   b) doubtful   c) late   d) overt   e) ambitious   22.___

23. copyright : book : : _____ : _____
   a) buyer   b) seller   c) patent   d) slogan   e) invention   23.___

24. Saturday : week : : _____ : _____
   a) day   b) calendar   c) year   d) late   e) October   24.___

25. peninsula : continent : : _____ : _____
   a) lake   b) mountain   c) ocean   d) bay   e) isthmus   25.___

Part G ◆ WORD PARTS

DIRECTIONS ◆ The list below includes words with common prefixes, roots, or suffixes. Look at each word part and the examples. Then write the meaning of the word part on the blank. Do not mark the short line at the right of each item. Save it for scoring later on.

WORD PART	EXAMPLES	MEANING	
1. omni	omnivorous, omnibus	_____	1.__
2. post	postdate, postscript	_____	2.__
3. geo	geography, geology	_____	3.__
4. tele	telephone, telegraph	_____	4.__
5. auto	automotive, autograph	_____	5.__
6. inter	international, interfere	_____	6.__
7. sub	subway, submarine	_____	7.__
8. re	reclaim, renew	_____	8.__
9. chron	chronological, chronic	_____	9.__
10. bene	benefactor, beneficiary	_____	10.__
11. fore	foresight, forethought	_____	11.__
12. mono	monologue, monotone	_____	12.__
13. in	infirm, indecent, inactive	_____	13.__
14. fy, ify	magnify, fortify	_____	14.__
15. il	illegible, illegal	_____	15.__
16. tran, trans	transport, transcribe	_____	16.__
17. anti	antidote, antiseptic	_____	17.__
18. hood	statehood, childhood	_____	18.__
19. less	thoughtless, witless	_____	19.__
20. ate	activate, animate	_____	20.__
21. port	import, portable	_____	21.__
22. arium, orium	auditorium, aquarium	_____	22.__
23. vert, vers	revert, version	_____	23.__
24. a, ab	atypical, abnormal	_____	24.__
25. circum	circumnavigate	_____	25.__

Part H ✦ LISTING SYNONYMS AND ANTONYMS

1. Write five words that mean the same, or nearly the same, as *skillful*.

   _____ _____ _____

   _____ _____ 1. ___

2. Write five words that have the general meaning of *take*.

   _____ _____ _____

   _____ _____ 2. ___

3. Write five words with the same general meaning as *old*.

   _____ _____ _____

   _____ _____ 3. ___

4. Write five words with about the same meaning as *kind* (*gentle*).

   _____ _____ _____

   _____ _____ 4. ___

5. Write five words each meaning the opposite of *small*.

   _____ _____ _____

   _____ _____ 5. ___

Part I ✦ SPELLING

1. Change *liquid* into a verb meaning "to make liquid." _____   1. ___

2. Change *acquit* to a noun. _____   2. ___

3. Change *occur* to a noun. _____   3. ___

4. Write a word beginning with the letter *p* that means "at the same distance apart everywhere." _____   4. ___

5. Write a word beginning with the syllable *em* and meaning "disturb (a person), make self-conscious." _____   5. ___

6. Write a word beginning with the letter *g* and meaning "measure," or "to measure," or "an instrument for measuring." _____   6. ___

7. Write a word beginning with the letter *a* and meaning "one who does something for pleasure rather than for pay," or "one who does something rather poorly."

   _____   7. ___

8. Write a word beginning with *w* and meaning "unearthly, mysterious." "We were wakened by a _____ shriek." 8.___

9. Write a verb beginning with the letter *p* and meaning "predict" or "foretell." _____ 9.___

10. Change *propel* to a noun meaning "a device that propels."

_____ 10.___

Part J ✦ MEANINGS OF GENERAL WORDS

DIRECTIONS ✦ From each group below select the lettered word or phrase which most nearly corresponds in meaning to the *italicized* word. Write the letter on the blank at the right. Work rapidly.

1. *diffident* at times

   a) fierce, savage
   b) artistic, clever
   c) misunderstood
   d) shy, retiring 1.___

2. with *therapeutic* value

   a) financial
   b) curative
   c) disciplinary
   d) literary 2.___

3. to *convene*

   a) assemble
   b) defend
   c) recall
   d) make comfortable 3.___

4. *sporadic* attacks

   a) wild, disorganized
   b) occurring now and then
   c) aerial
   d) political 4.___

5. make a *memorandum*

   a) informal record
   b) debut
   c) great name
   d) recording machine 5.___

6. no longer an *alien*

   a) foreigner
   b) minor
   c) chauffeur
   d) enemy 6.___

7. no *tangible* effect

   a) harmful
   b) helpful
   c) real, definite
   d) curative 7.___

8. known for his *mendacity*

    a) wealth   c) generosity
    b) habit of lying   d) physical strength   8.___

9. to *lubricate* the machinery

    a) grease   c) replace
    b) repair   d) test   9.___

10. usually *tractable*

    a) well mannered   c) grammatical
    b) easy to deal with   d) industrious   10.___

11. neither acute nor *chronic*

    a) spread by contact   c) very severe
    b) long lasting   d) infectious   11.___

12. not apt to *deteriorate*

    a) depart   c) disagree
    b) remember   d) grow worse   12.___

13. a powerful *adversary*

    a) opponent   c) athlete
    b) ruler   d) disciplinarian   13.___

14. occasional *insomnia*

    a) forgetfulness   c) sleeplessness
    b) fear   d) hysteria   14.___

15. regarded as a *novice*

    a) threat   c) expert
    b) beginner   d) colleague   15.___

16. began to *reminisce*

    a) grow better   c) stutter
    b) talk about the past   d) raise questions   16.___

17. with *covert* glances

    a) secret   c) friendly
    b) fearful   d) curious   17.___

18. demanding *suffrage*

    a) medical care   c) the right to vote
    b) pay increases   d) better housing   18.___

19. an admirable *principal*

   a) fundamental belief
   b) general plan

   c) chief person
   d) policy

   19.___

20. always *voracious*

   a) ravenous
   b) quarrelsome

   c) mysterious
   d) wholesome

   20.___

21. a *bucolic* life

   a) monotonous
   b) physically active

   c) pastoral; rustic
   d) well planned

   21.___

22. known as a *gregarious* person

   a) fond of being with others
   b) eager to learn

   c) sports loving
   d) talkative

   22.___

23. a *precarious* undertaking

   a) costly
   b) strange, grotesque

   c) courageous
   d) risky

   23.___

24. a *diminutive* creature

   a) untamed, wild
   b) tiny

   c) self-satisfied
   d) industrious

   24.___

25. *adamant* in his stand
   a) unyielding
   b) unfair

   c) pompous
   d) prejudiced

   25.___

26. with a *pessimistic* prediction

   a) gloomy
   b) secret

   c) light-hearted
   d) stupid

   26.___

27. and no *bouillon*

   a) thin, clear soup
   b) bars of gold or silver

   c) currency
   d) mayonnaise

   27.___

28. the *overbearing* attitude

   a) pastoral, rural
   b) urban

   c) domineering
   d) penitent

   28.___

29. a *cardiac* condition

   a) abnormal
   b) heart

   c) painful
   d) abdominal

   29.___

14

30. a *symptom* to be watched

    a) performer   c) program

    b) sign, indication   d) political candidate   30.___

31. receive a *dividend*

    a) announcement   c) receipt

    b) advertisement   d) share of the profits   31.___

32. down the *runway*

    a) exercise field   c) landing strip for planes

    b) leakage   d) plane with two wings   32.___

33. with *negotiable* assets

    a) of doubtful worth   c) additional

    b) valuable   d) transferable   33.___

34. searching for an *antidote*

    a) remedy   c) lost mine

    b) fortune   d) pain reliever   34.___

35. to provide *collateral*

    a) proof   c) payment

    b) additional security   d) money lent at interest   35.___

36. to take a *census*

    a) numbering of the population   c) vote

    b) account of assets   d) sampling   36.___

37. become a *lessee*

    a) person to whom a lease is   c) purchaser

       granted   d) guarantor

    b) beneficiary   37.___

38. unusually *taciturn*

    a) resentful   c) buoyant

    b) unwilling to talk   d) cooperative   38.___

39. *eligible* to take the position

    a) eager   c) qualified

    b) unwilling   d) unprepared   39.___

40. a *versatile* genius

    a) conceited   c) conversational

    b) mathematical   d) many-sided   40.___

41. equipped with a *semaphore*

    a) typewriter   c) carburetor
    b) apparatus for signaling   d) brake   41.___

42. speak to the *proprietor*

    a) owner   c) actuary
    b) manager   d) beneficiary   42.___

43. and *reimburse* him

    a) inform   c) patronize
    b) thank   d) repay   43.___

44. *superfluous* words

    a) descriptive   c) persuasive
    b) coined on the moment   d) needless   44.___

45. to *maneuver* the car

    a) mishandle   c) purchase
    b) repair   d) operate skillfully   45.___

46. to *placate* the customer

    a) repay   c) soothe the anger of
    b) compliment   d) promise   46.___

47. to their *habitat*

    a) customary diet   c) riding costume
    b) dwelling place   d) conference   47.___

48. *ingenuous* remarks

    a) clever, witty   c) simple, innocent
    b) satirical   d) discourteous   48.___

49. an *archaic* word

    a) colorful   c) confusing
    b) technical   d) no longer in use   49.___

50. hire a *craftsman*

    a) skilled workman   c) foreman
    b) apprentice   d) contractor   50.___

The key is on page 184.

Part		Possible score	Your score
A	Vocations and Industries	10	_____
B	Specialists	10	_____
C	Nouns from Tomorrow's Jobs	10	_____
D	Words Often Confused	10	_____
E	Getting the Meaning from Context	20	_____
F	Analogies	25	_____
G	Word Parts	25	_____
H	Listing Synonyms and Antonyms	25	_____
I	Spelling	10	_____
J	Meanings of General Words	50	_____
		Total (195)	_____

PERSONAL INVENTORY

FACTORS RELATING TO YOUR WORD COMPETENCE

Word Interest

Have you a strong and continuing interest in words?

General words? _____

Words of special importance in your work or in a course you are taking? _____

Words with whimsical origins? _____

Word Attack

Do you tend to grasp readily the meanings of new words you encounter in reading or listening? _____

Have you a systematic plan for mastering the meanings of strange words? _____

Do you keep your vocabulary viable so that it grows and develops as your interests expand? _____

Have you a systematic plan for mastering the spelling of strange words? _____

Do you make regular use of your dictionary or Thesaurus? _____

Approximately how many new words have you learned in the last two weeks? _____

Write down four of these words.

_____   _____

_____   _____

How did you learn them?

_____

_____

_____

_____

Word Usage

In writing and speaking, do you direct your attention to the choice of suitable words? _____

Vision

Is your vision satisfactory for the clear perception of words? _____

SELF-APPRAISAL

On the basis of your various test results and your answers to the questions of the inventory, write a concise self-appraisal. How good is your word competence? In what ways do you wish to improve?

Section Two

manufacturing	the conversion of raw materials into finished products. Manufacturing today is concerned with the production of countless diverse products—foods, textiles, apparel, chemicals, automobiles, aircraft, steel, and typewriters, to name just a few.
trade, merchandising	the buying, pricing, display, advertising, selling, and servicing of marketable products.
transportation	the conveyance of products and people from one place to another by ship, train, plane, or truck.
construction	the building, maintenance, and repair of all types of structures, such as houses, factories, public buildings, offices, roads, dams, and bridges.
the services	occupations concerned with the transformation of human effort into ministration to human needs rather than into goods. Included are such varied callings as dental and medical practice, library work, teaching, child care, and cosmetology.
public utilities	industries which provide gas, electricity, water, telephone service, and so on.
mining	the extraction of metallic ores and fuels from the ground.
agriculture	the operation and management of farms.
conservation	the management, development, and protection of valuable lands and their resources—timber, water, wildlife, forage, and recreational opportunities, for example.
the professions	occupations requiring advanced education and specialized training. Medicine, dentistry, teaching, law, architecture, and the ministry are all professions.
government work	occupations of many kinds requiring many different levels of education, training, and skill, and all essential for the conduct of federal, state, and local governments.

IMPROVING WORD KNOWLEDGE

SUGGESTIONS FOR INDEPENDENT WORK

English is by far the largest of all languages.[2] Some of its words have been coined, but the great majority have been adopted from other languages, chiefly Anglo-Saxon, Latin, and Greek. From Anglo-Saxon we get the strong, simple, everyday words we all know—words like *come, good, this, that,* and *thanks.* From Latin and Greek we get many of our difficult words and technical terms.

[1] Not all of the important fields are listed.

[2] Gerald W. Johnson, *Our English Heritage* (Philadelphia: J. B. Lippincott Co., 1949), pp. 115–136.

But there is hardly a language on earth from which we have not borrowed. From Spanish we have words like *pueblo, cork, adobe, mosquito,* and *cigar;* from French, *chassis, chauffeur, restaurant, parole,* and others. *Opossum, raccoon, skunk,* and *persimmon* have come from the North American Indians; *yodel, semester, poodle,* and *kindergarten* are of German origin; and from Italian we have words like *miniature, umbrella, piano,* and *regatta.*

Large though it is, the language continues to grow. We get new words from science and technology, from business, and from the steady stream of inventions and discoveries—words like *telecast, transistor, antibiotics,* and *subsonics.* We turn people's names into nouns and verbs: *pasteurize,* for example, comes from French scientist Louis Pasteur. Occasionally we give status to slang: *cheese, bunkum,* and *flabbergast* are three examples of such terms that have made their ways into the dictionary.

With a stockpile so vast, no single selection of reasonable length can meet in full the needs of all people, or even the needs of the same individual throughout the course of his life. Core lists are often invaluable in pointing out words of key importance in communication, but the total list for any individual should reflect his occupation, his interests and hobbies, his goals, and even the part of the world in which he lives. The command of words should be viable—capable always of change and growth.

EXTENDING AND ENRICHING
WORD COMPETENCE

1. *Be on the alert for words of importance to you.*

If you seek them out, you will learn them rapidly. If you aren't interested, you won't make much progress.

Words can be fun, and you may enjoy occasional oddities like *quirl* and *wysty.* As a rule, however, concentrate on words of everyday importance. If you look toward a career in advertising, make sure of the precise definitions of such words as *brochure, italics, format, pica,* and *caption.* For work in insurance and real estate turn your attention to *abstract, negotiable, indemnity, quitclaim,* and related terms; for architecture and building look to such words as *buttress, cornice, mortise,* and *portico.*

At one time nearly everyone's goal involved obtaining and holding a single job. In recent years, however, scientific knowledge has been accumulating at a steadily increasing rate, and, in consequence, jobs have been subject to almost continual change.

Employment and promotion today depend in important measure upon adaptability. A key ingredient is competence in understanding—precisely—explanations, instructions, and directives related to the job.

Attention should also be given to important general words in common use:

adamant in his stand	with *ominous* overtones
no known *panacea*	and discover *latent* ability
to *malign* a friend	with a financial *incentive*

2. *Try first to arrive independently at the meanings of strange words.*

Often the context will provide the clues.

> At the time his mother was 33, his father, 63. The thirty-year *disparity* in his parents' ages did not contribute to a happy home life.

Word parts may also suggest the meaning; the parts *syn* and *chron* point directly to the meaning of *synchronize.*

3. *If a new word is of more than passing interest, check your inferences.*

Look up the definition (or definitions) in a dictionary. Note the pronunciation; look also for spelling alternatives.

4. *Keep a card file.*

For each word to be added to your active vocabulary, make out a separate card. On one side write the word and indicate its pronunciation, then add a phrase or short sentence to illustrate its use. On the reverse side, record at least one meaning.

5. *Make a systematic effort to master the data.*

Study intensively but keep the study periods short. Repeat the process at least once a day.

Look at the word and try to recall the meaning. Then check. Once you have gone through the pack, proceed in reverse: look at the meaning and try to recall the word. Always keep in mind the intent to remember. Make a clear distinction between passive and active knowledge.

Test your spelling. Chances are good that your work in mastering the meaning will also result in mastery of the spelling. But if uncertainties persist, single out the word for special attention.

Keep the card pack to a reasonable size. Shuffle the cards often.

6. *Sharpen and refine your knowledge of words already partly familiar.*

Try your skill at composing definitions. To define, of course, means "to set the limits of." What, for example, is a *syllable?* The statement, "A syllable is a part of a word," is insufficient; it fails to make clear the difference between a letter and a syllable.

Once you have a definition that seems satisfactory to you, check with your dictionary. *Work for preciseness by seeking out synonyms and antonyms.* Where groups of words are related in meaning but not identical, make clear the distinctions. Examples: *tour, jaunt, trip, cruise, pilgrimage, excursion, flight.*

Distinguish between words commonly confused. Ingenious and *ingenuous* are examples: so, also, are *sensual* and *sensuous.*

7. *Use the new words repeatedly in your speaking and writing.*

BUILDING SPELLING COMPETENCE

Spelling calls for exact study. To be acceptable, spelling must be correct. Many approaches have identified accuracy with industry and have placed a premium upon slow, detailed exploration and time-consuming repetition.

But industry of itself is largely without virtue.

Laboratory studies of eye movements have shown that at any academic level the number of pauses is less for the good speller than for the poor one; the average study span is broader and the average study time, shorter.

The procedure of individuals who find spelling easy varies with spelling maturity. The young learner, unfamiliar with the common letter combinations and their functions, tends to explore a new word in detail. After an introductory period many of the letter combinations lose their strangeness, and he is able to move ahead with increased regularity, speed, and breadth of grasp. Typically, the good speller soon learns to differentiate between hard spots and easy ones; he reserves his special attention for those areas he finds troublesome.

In your own study, work *judiciously* to increase your rate of mastery. One dividend will be the ability to pick up quickly the spelling of many new words during the normal course of reading and study.

Be cautious in your reliance on spelling rules. One rule states that a final silent *e* should be dropped if a syllable beginning with a vowel is added: for example, *come, coming, move, moving*. But there are exceptions—*serviceable, marriageable, manageable*.

Another rule states that when *ei* or *ie* has the sound of *ee*, the *ei* should be used after *c*, the *ie* after other consonants. But here again are exceptions; e.g., *leisure, neither,* and *seize*.

Because few, if any, rules are without exceptions, it seems preferable to learn each word as a distinct item.

1. *Look at each new word as a whole or in large units.*

Avoid the letter-by-letter procedure and reliance upon unneeded repetitions.

2. *Seek out the hard spots and give them the attention they need.*

3. *Fuse the parts into a unified word, once the difficulties seem to be out of the way.*

Look at the word, with firm intent to remember the correct spelling NOW. Don't come to rely upon "the next time."

4. *Check your knowledge.*

Write the word immediately and from memory. If there are any errors, make corrections without delay. Keep in mind the goal of rapid study with a high standard of efficiency.

5. *Be on the alert for suitable opportunities to use the words in your writing.*

List Two ✦ GENERAL WORDS

DIRECTIONS ✦ Read these words aloud. Make sure you can pronounce them.

WORD	SYLLABLES	PRONUNCIATION
formidable	for′ mi da ble	**FOR′** mi da bel
reminisce	rem′ i nisce′	rem′ i **NISS′**
exotic	ex ot′ ic	eg **ZOT′** ik
novice	nov′ ice	**NOV′** iss
audacity	au dac′ i ty	aw **DASS′** i tee
vindicate	vin′ di cate	**VIN′** di kate
tractable	trac′ ta ble	**TRAC′** ta bel
taciturn	tac′ i turn	**TASS′** i turn
synonym	syn′ o nym	**SIN′** o nim
antonym	an′ to nym	**AN′** toe nim

MEANINGS³

formidable	hard to overcome; hard to deal with: *The second opponent was more formidable than the first.*
reminisce	think about or talk about events or experiences of the past: *Businessmen often get together to reminisce about their football days.*
exotic	from a strange country; not native; foreign: *Exotic rugs brought out the beauty of the room.*
novice	beginner; one who is new to what he is doing: *The novice can learn by watching the expert.*
audacity	boldness; effrontery; assertiveness: *No one in the group had the audacity to contradict the branch manager.*
vindicate	clear of suspicion, dishonor, or charge of wrongdoing: *He knew that the letter would vindicate him and prove his right to the money.*
tractable	easily managed or controlled; easy to deal with: *Most dogs are tractable if they are treated well.*
taciturn	not given to much talking; speaking little: *He was a taciturn man and it was hard to predict how he would vote.*
synonym	word that has the same meaning or nearly the same meaning as another: *"Prudent" and "cautious" are synonyms.*
antonym	word that means the opposite of another: *"Hot" and "cold" are antonyms.*

³ Not all meanings are listed.

homonym	word having the same pronunciation as another, but a different meaning: *"Sent" and "scent" are homonyms.*
abrupt	sudden: *The long tale of suffering came to an abrupt end.*
dubious	uncertain; doubtful: *When the golfer saw the new course, he was dubious about his chances of winning the tournament.*
dissent	disagree; think differently; express a different point of view: *If your feeling is one of dissent, you can express it through your vote.*
confidant	person trusted with the secret and private information of another: *There were some who felt that the new Senator was a confidant of the President.*
skeptical	inclined to doubt; not believing easily: *The manufacturers made great claims for the new drug, but the doctors were skeptical.*
carnivorous	flesh-eating: *Tigers are carnivorous animals.*
decrepit	broken down and weakened by age: *At seventy-five years of age, he was neither blind nor decrepit.*
cavalcade	procession of persons riding on horses or in vehicles: *The cavalcade moved slowly down the tree-lined streets of the town.*
equine	of a horse; horselike: *The stablekeeper was an expert on equine health.*
diffident	shy; lacking in self-confidence: *He was a well-informed young man, but too diffident to speak before a large group.*
squander	waste; lavish: *It was the fear of many that the heirs would squander the entire estate.*
diligent	active; sedulous, attentive, hard-working: *She was a diligent accountant.*
dormitory	building with many sleeping rooms: *The university maintained one large dormitory for men.*
restrict	keep within limits; confine: *The shops are restricted to the downtown area.*
habitat	area where a plant or animal lives: *The tiger was returned to his native habitat in Asia.*

Exercise 1 ◆ ADAPTING WORD FORMS

DIRECTIONS ◆ Complete each sentence by writing in the word that is required. Save the numbered blank at the right for your scoring later on.

1. Change *abrupt* to an adverb. Dizziness overcame him, and he cut off his

   speech _____.   1.___

2. Change *taciturn* to a noun. He read much but talked little; he was famous

   for his _____.   2.___

3. Change *tractable* to a related word meaning "not easily managed." Most of

   the students agreed, but a few were indifferent or even _____.   3.___

4. Change *reminisce* to a noun. The author has written about his famous father. This is a book of _____. 4.___

5. What is the noun form of *skeptical?* The scientist does not believe readily. He tends to be a _____. 5.___

6. Change *carnivorous* to a noun. The lion is a _____. 6.___

7. Change *decrepit* to a noun. Fortunately, great age is not always marked by

_____. 7.___

8. Change *dissent* to a noun. The meeting was a noisy one reflecting great ____

_____. 8.___

9. Change *audacity* to an adjective. There was nothing diffident about him; he was a forceful, _____ man. 9.___

10. Change *vindicate* to a noun. The letters in the safe provided the facts that led to his _____. 10.___

The key is on page 186.   Number of correct answers _____

Exercise 2 ✦ FINDING ANTONYMS

DIRECTIONS ✦ An antonym is a word that means the opposite of another word. *Disperse, adjourn,* and *dissolve* are antonyms of *convene.* Look at the key word at the left. Then, from the group at the right, select the one that is opposite in meaning. Write its letter on the blank.

1. novice   a) beginner   b) expert   c) newcomer   d) trainee   1.___

2. taciturn   a) quiet   b) stingy   c) moody   d) talkative   2.___

3. dissent   a) discuss   b) argue   c) agree   d) insult   3.___

4. abrupt   a) steep   b) sharp   c) rude   d) gradual   4.___

5. dubious   a) certain   b) puzzled   c) thoughtful d) rude   5.___

6. exotic   a) native   b) costly   c) modern   d) foreign   6.___

7. tractable   a) eager   b) bright   c) strong   d) obstinate   7.___

8. vindicate   a) absolve   b) acquit   c) clear   d) convict   8.___

The key is on page 186.   Number of correct answers _____

26

Exercise 3 ◆ WRITING HOMONYMS

DIRECTIONS ◆ A homonyn is a word having the same pronunciation as another, but a different meaning. *Meat* and *meet* are homonyms. On the blank in the center, write the homonym for the key word at the left. Save the blank at the right for scoring.

1. weight _____ 1.___

2. piece _____ 2.___

3. hole _____ 3.___

4. principle _____ 4.___

5. waste _____ 5.___

6. plain _____ 6.___

7. our _____ 7.___

8. residence _____ 8.___

The key is on page 186.   Number of correct answers _____

Exercise 4 ◆ FINDING SYNONYMS

DIRECTIONS ◆ A synonym is a word that means the same, or nearly the same, as another word. *Grumble, deplore,* and *bewail* are synonyms of *complain.* Think about the word at the left. Then, from the group at the right, select the one that is nearest in meaning. Write its letter on the blank.

1. exotic	a) tropical	b) foreign	c) costly	d) fragile	1.___
2. dissent	a) examine	b) debate	c) punish	d) disagree	2.___
3. audacity	a) cost	b) courage	c) strength	d) boldness	3.___
4. dubious	a) doubtful	b) quiet	c) sure	d) dishonest	4.___
5. novice	a) expert	b) plumber	c) beginner	d) carpenter	5.___
6. abrupt	a) sudden	b) gradual	c) rough	d) painful	6.___
7. vindicate	a) acquit	b) accuse	c) prove	d) convict	7.___
8. tractable	a) tardy	b) witty	c) easily managed	d) muddy	8.___

The key is on page 186.   Number of correct answers _____

Exercise 5 ✦ WRITING SYNONYMS

DIRECTIONS ✦ Write two synonyms for each of the key words at the left.

1. error _____ _____ 1. ___
2. save _____ _____ 2. ___
3. accept _____ _____ 3. ___
4. commend _____ _____ 4. ___
5. journey _____ _____ 5. ___
6. strength _____ _____ 6. ___
7. keep _____ _____ 7. ___
8. scatter _____ _____ 8. ___
9. patience _____ _____ 9. ___
10. fear _____ _____ 10. ___

The key is on page 186.   Possible score, 20   Your score _____

Exercise 6 ✦ WRITING ANTONYMS

DIRECTIONS ✦ Write two antonyms for each of the key words at the left.

1. careful _____ _____ 1. ___
2. accept _____ _____ 2. ___
3. gloom _____ _____ 3. ___
4. fragile _____ _____ 4. ___
5. imaginary _____ _____ 5. ___
6. linger _____ _____ 6. ___
7. punish _____ _____ 7. ___
8. rise _____ _____ 8. ___
9. sour _____ _____ 9. ___
10. tighten _____ _____ 10. ___

The key is on page 186.   Possible score, 20   Your score _____

28

Exercise 7 ◆ GETTING THE MEANING
FROM THE CONTEXT

D I R E C T I O N S ◆ Read each passage and decide on the meaning of the *italicized* word as it is used there. Then write the meaning concisely on the blank. At this time, do not refer to a dictionary or thesaurus.

1. The population of Australia is predominantly Anglo-Saxon and of British origin. But its general nature is changing slowly with the continuing *influx* of migrants from continental Europe.

_____   1.___

2. Here we have a *paradox*. Difficulty in settling down to work often wrecks good resolutions and plans, but the deliberate effort to follow a schedule will gradually improve the ability to settle down to work. Effectiveness here is largely a matter of habit.

_____   2.___

3. Today one may find the same conveniences of modern life in certain parts of Alaska that are found elsewhere in the country. Many visitors who tour only the modern cities are unaware of the fact that a vast *disparity* exists between the level of living of Alaska's "newcomers" and that of the aboriginal population. In fact, the disparity is so great that the state may be thought of as two widely different realms.

_____   3.___

4. Part, at least, of the accomplishments of science are due to the care taken in describing each object or event in the most precise way possible. Where no satisfactory word exists for naming something, a new term must be invented. Occasionally loose usage is recognized and old terms are discarded in favor of newer ones that avoid the *ambiguity*.

_____   4.___

5. Chances of advancement for the fireman generally depend upon his position on the promotion list. This is determined by his rating on a written examination, his work as a fireman, and his seniority. Throughout his service he continues to study fire prevention, *incendiarism,* and related subjects to improve his performance on the job.

_____   5.___

6. It is important to keep in mind that any conclusions about the economic future of the country rest upon certain assumptions at this time. One is that no *cataclysmic* events will occur—a war, for example, or a severe depression.

_____   6.___

7. What are the chief aspects of American society that influence the nature of American democratic government? First of all, the United States is a land of infinite geographical *diversity*. Consider our climate and our land: our nation embraces burning deserts, mountain ranges, humid areas drenched with rain, dust bowls, and thousands of miles of coastline. Second, America is the "melting pot" of the people of the world.

_____   7.___

8. His older brother Radford, now nearly seventy, has become one of the nation's most respected judges—a man with true impact on the law. Yet despite his enormous *prestige* in his profession, he is virtually unknown to the general public.

_____   8.___

9. Dependent upon the sea and the tundra for food and clothing, the Eskimos have highly developed techniques for fishing and hunting, and the number of their skills is now being *augmented* by modern inventions—steel fishhooks, semiautomatic rifles, nylon fish nets, and outboard motors.

_____   9.___

10. The communities of advanced food-gathering peoples are small villages, with a few large market villages. These bands of communities are economically self-sufficient. They are also *autonomous* politically, although they come together now and then for the consideration of matters of common importance.

_____   10.___

11. We fix 1910 as the year in which *agrarian* culture in the United States gave way to industrial culture. For the first time in history, more people earned their livings in industry than in agriculture.

_____   11.___

12. There was nothing *surreptitious* about the departure of the foreign ships. They left the Bay at noontime in bright sunlight and their going was manifest to everyone there ashore.

_____   12.___

13. Through advertisements published in newspapers and magazines, broadcast on the radio, shown on television, displayed on billboards, sent through the mail, or even written in smoke in the sky, businessmen try to reach *potential* customers and persuade them to buy their products or services.

_____   13.___

14. The load carried varies greatly from stream to stream. First, it differs because of the rainfall. Then, differences in kinds of rock affect the amount of *sediment*. Streams from watersheds composed of fine, windblown soil contribute large amounts of sediment with every rainfall. But streams draining from hard rocks carry very little sediment.

_____   14.___

15. Membership in a high class or caste carries distinct social advantages, but membership in the lower strata involves real disadvantages. A member of a lower class group must work harder for less *remuneration*, and he has little, if any, chance for any inheritance.

_____ 15.___

If your answer at any time differs from the one given in the key, and you think it is correct, check with your dictionary.

Exercise 8 ◆ ANALOGIES

DIRECTIONS ◆ Below is a list of 18 words. On each blank that follows write in the word from the list that best completes the analogy.

EXAMPLE ◆ day : light : : night : darkness
Here the first two words have about the same relationship as the second two. Day is to light as night is to darkness. An analogy is a resemblance in the relationship between groups of words.

dentist : teeth : : oculist : eyes
bat : baseball : : racquet : tennis
horse : equine : : fox : vulpine

affluent	dexterity	lethal
anecdote	elated	novice
asset	entice	prefix
audacity	extinguish	reminiscence
copyright	fortitude	uneasy
cupidity	futile	upright

1. weakness : strength : : clumsiness : _____ 1.___

2. _____ : suffix : : beginning : ending 2.___

3. deadly : _____ : : sound : valid 3.___

4. opulent : _____ : : poor : destitute 4.___

5. shyness : diffidence : : boldness : _____ 5.___

6. _____ : story : : remedy : antidote 6.___

7. dejected : discouraged : : _____ : joyful 7.___

8. remember : memory : : reminisce : _____ 8.___

9. repel : _____ : : lazy : diligent 9.___

10. expert : _____ : : opponent : ally 10.___

11. debit : credit : : liability : _____   11.___

12. fragile : robust : : prostrate : _____   12.___

13. _____ : ignite : : quench : kindle   13.___

14. greed : _____ : : motley : variegated   14.___

15. cowardice : _____ : : distress : comfort   15.___

The key is on page 187.   Possible score, 15   Your score _____

Exercise 9 ◆ REVIEW

DIRECTIONS ◆ Read each item. Then select the best meaning for the *italicized* word and enter its letter on the blank at the right. Work from memory.

1. our most *taciturn* president

    a) vigorous   c) scholarly
    b) outgoing, talkative   d) reserved, silent   1.___

2. searching for an *antonym*

    a) long-time career   c) word opposite in meaning
    b) excuse, reason   d) descriptive term   2.___

3. no known *confidant*

    a) person trusted with one's   c) fiction writer
       secrets   d) embezzler
    b) witness   3.___

4. a *skeptical* attitude

    a) disinterested   c) fearful
    b) doubting   d) contemptuous   4.___

5. a *tractable* prisoner

    a) vicious, spiteful   c) starving
    b) easily managed   d) newly arrived   5.___

6. no opportunity there for a *novice*

    a) foreigner   c) electrician
    b) apprentice   d) architect   6.___

7. an *abrupt* decision

    a) sudden   c) final
    b) unexpected   d) tentative   7.___

8. began to *reminisce*

    a) complain bitterly   c) weaken, falter

    b) talk of the past   d) make a new decision   8.___

9. the *audacity* of the request

    a) foresightedness   c) boldness

    b) modesty   d) thoughtlessness   9.___

10. *exotic* merchandise

    a) shoddy   c) handmade

    b) costly   d) foreign   10.___

11. the *habitat* of tigers

    a) dwelling place   c) behavior, habits

    b) natural diet   d) zoological description   11.___

12. no longer *diffident*

    a) unconcerned   c) bashful

    b) attractive   d) talkative   12.___

13. *equine* behavior

    a) lazy, inactive   c) undisciplined

    b) like that of a horse   d) acceptable   13.___

14. of *dubious* worth

    a) uncertain   c) untested

    b) fabulous   d) well publicized   14.___

15. a *formidable* opponent

    a) menacing   c) aging

    b) untrained   d) conventional   15.___

The key is on page 187.

Number of correct answers _____

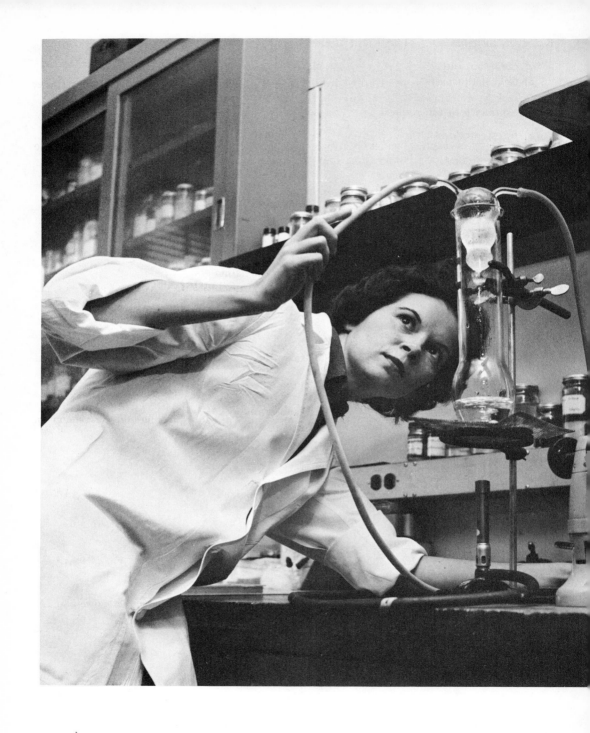

Section Three

COMMON WORD PARTS

Many English words are formed from Latin or Greek word parts. *Export,* for example, traces back to the Latin *ex,* "out," and *port,* "carry"; *postscript* is derived from *post,* "after," and *script,* "written."

Listed below are a few common word parts. Study their meanings. Then explore the everyday words that follow and think how they were formed.

pre-	before in time, place, order, rank	predict, prepay
mis-	wrong, wrongly, ill	mislead, misconduct
sub-	under, below, of lesser importance	subway, subhead
omni-	all	omnipotent, omnibus
trans-, tran-, tra-	across, over, beyond, through	transform, transatlantic
ex-	out, out from	exhale, extract

Exercise 10 ✦ IDENTIFYING MEANINGS THROUGH WORD PARTS

DIRECTIONS ✦ On the blank at the right, print the letter that identifies the best meaning.

1. based on *misinformation*

   a) rumor   c) facts
   b) inaccurate information   d) reasoning   1. ___

2. the *omnipresent* mosquitoes

   a) minute, tiny   c) tropical
   b) annoying   d) present everywhere   2. ___

3. to *exclude* vagrants

   a) shut out   c) shadow
   b) fine   d) encourage   3. ___

4. an *excerpt* from the speech

   a) idea   c) part taken out
   b) inference   d) line   4. ___

5. have no *premonition*

   a) cash on hand   c) uncertainty
   b) memory   d) forewarning   5. ___

6. *misplaced* confidence

    a) absolute   c) continuing

    b) given to the wrong person   d) well considered   6.___

7. in charge of the *submarine*

    a) hydroplane   c) ferry

    b) freighter   d) underwater vessel   7.___

8. *transcontinental* railroad

    a) high speed   c) out-of-date

    b) luxury   d) crossing a continent   8.___

9. at a *predetermined* time

    a) future   c) decided in advance

    b) widely publicized   d) convenient   9.___

10. the *misuse* of the word

    a) full meaning   c) effect

    b) origin   d) incorrect use   10.___

The key is on page 187.   Your score _____

Exercise 11 ✦ SUPPLYING THE WORDS DEFINED

DIRECTIONS ✦ Fill in the blanks, supplying the words defined. Use words with prefixes from this list. Make no marks now on the numbered blanks at the far right; save them for the scoring.

         pre-   sub-   trans-, tran-, tra-

         mis-   omni-   ex-

1. copy in handwriting or on the typewriter   _____   1.___

2. standing out above all others   _____   2.___

3. dig up from one place and plant in another   _____   3.___

4. eating all kinds of food   _____   4.___

5. put under water   _____   5.___

6. bad behavior   _____   6.___

7. breathe out   _____   7.___

8. under normal   _____   8.___

The key is on page 187.   Your score _____

Exercise 12 ◆ SUPPLYING WORDS WITH
THE PREFIXES PROVIDED

DIRECTIONS ◆ Write three words (not used in Exercises 10 and 11) that begin with the prefix *pre-* and incorporate the general idea of "before" in time, place, order, or rank.

_____   _____   _____

DIRECTIONS ◆ Write three words (not used in the Exercises) that begin with the prefix *mis-* and incorporate the idea of "wrong, ill, bad, badly, wrongly."

_____   _____   _____

DIRECTIONS ◆ Write three words (not used in the Exercises) that begin with the prefix *trans-* and incorporate the idea of "across, over, through, beyond" or "on the other side of."

_____   _____   _____

The key is on page 188.   Number of correct answers _____

AFFIXES AND COMBINING FORMS—
A WARNING

A list of prefixes, suffixes, and combining forms is provided for your convenience. Learning word parts in isolation is largely a waste of time, since it cannot be depended upon to contribute to the understanding of new words either alone or in context. Properly developed, however, the learning of word parts is an invaluable aid in increasing both the range and depth of your knowledge.

For best results, begin with the analysis of a few words already partly familiar and with groups of words related in origin and in meaning. Then, later, make use of your knowledge in trying to arrive independently at the meanings of new words. Make use of it also in fixing in mind the distinctions between pairs of words commonly confused. *Intermural* and *intramural* are examples.

But always remember the long and varied history of the language and the apparent inconsistencies in words. The letters *pre* and *re* at the beginnings of words do not always constitute prefixes: *pretty, preach, real,* and *reach* are examples. Nor do the endings *age, al,* and *ize* always constitute suffixes: note *cage, rage, seal, meal,* and *size.*

Whenever a word is to be added to your active vocabulary, check your inference with the dictionary.

BASIC PREFIXES, SUFFIXES, AND ROOT WORDS

PREFIX	MEANING[1]	EXAMPLE
a-, an-	without, not	atypical
ab-	away, from	abnormal
ad-	to, toward	administer
amb-, ambi-	around, about	ambiguous
ante-	before	antedate
anti-	against	antidote
arch-	chief	archbishop
bene-	well, good	benefactor
cata-, cath-	down, downward	catacombs
circum-	around	circumnavigate
con-, com-	with, together	congregate
contra-	against	contradict
de-	down	depose
demi-	half	demitasse
dia-	through	diameter
dis-	not	dislike
dys-	ill, hard, unlike	dyslexia
ex-	out, from	exhale
eu-	well	eugenic
extra-	without, outside, beyond	extralegal
hemi-	half	hemisphere
hyper-	above, excessive	hyperactive
hypo-	under, insufficient	hypodermic
in-	in, into	inside
in-, im-	not	inactive, improper
infra-	lower	infrared
inter-	between	intercede
intra-	within	intramural
juxta-	next, near	juxtaposition
mal-	wrong, ill, bad	malform
mis-	wrong, ill	mislead

[1] Not all meanings are listed.

PREFIX	MEANING	EXAMPLE
multi-	many	multipolar
per-	through	perennial
peri-	around	perimeter
poly-	many	polygamy
post-	after	postscript
pre-	before	preheat
pro-	in front of	proscenium
pro-	before	prologue
re-	back, again	return
retro-	backward	retrogress
semi-	half	semiannually
sub-	under	submarine
super-	above, over	supernumerary
syn-, sym-	together	symphony
trans-	across	translate
un-	not	unreal
vice-	in place of	viceroy

SUFFIX	MEANING	EXAMPLE
-able, -ible	capable of, suitable for	durable, visible
-acy	quality or state of	piracy, privacy
-age	act or state of, place of abode	breakage, orphanage
-al	pertaining to	rental, abdominal
-ance, -ence	quality or state of	insurance, competence
-ant	quality of, one who	reliant, servant
-arium, -orium	place for	aquarium, auditorium
-ary	place for, pertaining to	dictionary, elementary
-ate	cause to be	activate, animate
-ation, -ition	indicating action, state of	creation, discoloration, condition
-esque	like in manner or style	picturesque
-cle, -icle	a diminutive ending	corpuscle, denticle
-ferous	full of, bearing	coniferous
-ful	abounding in	colorful
-ic	pertaining to	democratic, phonic

SUFFIX	MEANING	EXAMPLE
-fy, -ify	to make, to cause to be	fortify, magnify
-hood	state of, condition of	childhood, statehood
-ism	quality of, doctrine of	conservatism, Marxism
-ity, -ty	quality or state of	acidity, familiarity
-itis	inflammation of	appendicitis
-ive	quality of, that which	creative, suggestive
-ize	to make, give, practice	memorize
-ment	act or condition of	statement, attainment
-mony	resulting condition	testimony, parsimony
-or	person who, thing which	conqueror, generator
-ose, -ous	full of	verbose, porous
-oid	in the form of	ovoid
-osis	condition, state, progress	hypnosis, psychosis
-tude	quality or degree of	solitude, altitude

LATIN ROOT	MEANING	EXAMPLE
aequus	equal	equilateral, equinox
amare, amatum	to love	amiable, amateur
annus	year	annual, annalist
audire, auditum	to hear	audible, auditorium
capere, captum	to take	capture, accept
caput	head	caption, decapitate
facere, factum	to make, to do	manufacture
dicere, dictum	to say, to speak	diction, edict
loqui, locutum	to speak	eloquence, colloquial
lucere	to be light	translucent, elucidate
medius	middle	mediate
mittere, missum	to send	admit, permit
manus	hand	manual, manuscript
omnis	all	omnipotent
ponere, positum	to place	post, depose
populus	people	popular
portare, portatum	to carry	porter, portable
quaerere, quaesitum	to ask, to question	inquire, acquire
rogare, rogatum	to ask	interrogate

LATIN ROOT	MEANING	EXAMPLE
scribere, scriptum	to write	postscript, describe
sentire, sensum	to feel	sense, dissent, consent
specere, spectum	to look at	inspect, introspect
tempus	time	temporary
spirare, spiratum	to breathe	inspire, conspire
torquere, tortum	to turn	distort, torture
venire, ventum	to go, to arrive	adventure, convention
vertere, versum	to turn	revert, universe
videre, visum	to see	visible, supervisor

GREEK ROOT[2]	MEANING	EXAMPLE
amphi-, ambi-	both	amphibious, ambidextrous
aster	star	asterisk, astronomy
bios (bio-)	life	biology, biography
chroma (chrom-)	color	chromosome
chronos (chrono-)	time	chronological
derma	skin	dermatologist, hypodermic
ethnos (ethno-)	race, tribe	ethnology
gamos (-gamy, -gamous)	marriage, union	bigamous, monogamy
genos (gene-)	race	genetics, genealogy
geo	earth	geology, geography
graphein (-graph)	to write	photograph, polygraph
helios (helio-)	sun, light	heliotropism
kryptos (crypto-)	hidden, secret	cryptogram, cryptic
kratus (-crat)	member of group or class	plutocrat, democrat
logos (log-, -logy)	speech, study of	prologue, sociology
metron (-meter, metro-)	measure	barometer, metronoscope
morphe (morph-, -morphic)	form	morphology
osteon (osteo-)	bone	osteomyelitis
pater	father	paternal
pathos (patho-, -path)	suffering, feeling	pathogenic, psychopath
phagein (-phagy, -phageous)	to feed, consume	bacteriophage
philos (philo-, -phile)	loving	bibliophile, philanthropist

[2] Combining forms are given in parenthesis.

GREEK ROOT	MEANING	EXAMPLE
phobos (-phobe)	fear	Anglophobe
photos (photo-)	light	photograph
pneuma	wind, air	pneumatic
podos (-pod, -poda)	foot	tripod, hexapoda
pseudein (pseudo-)	to deceive	pseudonym
pyr (pyro-)	fire	pyrotechnical
soma (somat-)	body	psychosomatic
tele	distant	telephone
theos (theo-)	a god	theology
therme (thermo-, -therm)	heat	thermometer

Exercise 13 ✦ SPEED OF INTERPRETATION

DIRECTIONS ✦ The exercise is made up of familiar, everyday words. Place an X before each item that mentions a kind of occupation or a person whose occupation is indicated.

EXAMPLE ✦ ____ a chilly afternoon
 _X_ pay the cashier

Time yourself as you work. As soon as you finish the first 40 items, record your time and check your answers. Then go to the second 40 items. Try to work more rapidly and, at the same time, more accurately.

START ✦

- ___ 1. vines and foliage
- ___ 2. point of view
- ___ 3. yesterday
- ___ 4. a tip for the porter
- ___ 5. repaired by the roofer
- ___ 6. waste of time
- ___ 7. go to school
- ___ 8. to a good teacher
- ___ 9. seeing is believing
- ___10. no small talent
- ___11. lunch table chatter
- ___12. honor and glory
- ___13. behind the trucker
- ___14. a true entertainer
- ___15. heard the broadcast
- ___16. shocking
- ___17. a delicate infant
- ___18. no ordinary broker
- ___19. the newest cars

START ✦

- ___ 1. weak and strong
- ___ 2. in agriculture
- ___ 3. six felines
- ___ 4. friends and enemies
- ___ 5. a child of poverty
- ___ 6. a radio broadcaster
- ___ 7. told the teletypist
- ___ 8. desist
- ___ 9. all living creatures
- ___10. an able manager
- ___11. well trained
- ___12. good with clerks
- ___13. and routemen
- ___14. now and then
- ___15. here and there
- ___16. informal dress
- ___17. no uniform
- ___18. repaired by the jeweler
- ___19. voice of the turtle

___ 20. ask the nurse		___ 20. the great decision	
___ 21. a forest conservationist		___ 21. spare a dime	
___ 22. a welcome promotion		___ 22. for forty years	
___ 23. with a pay raise		___ 23. a diesel mechanic	
___ 24. as a salesman		___ 24. school superintendent	
___ 25. he is alone		___ 25. a public utility	
___ 26. with his dinner		___ 26. alternately	
___ 27. no substitute		___ 27. no home, no friend	
___ 28. calling for a painter		___ 28. in salt water	
___ 29. over the weekend		___ 29. needed a glazier	
___ 30. in the sunshine		___ 30. another fireman	
___ 31. worn-out shoes		___ 31. on this planet	
___ 32. two detectives		___ 32. trained as a nurse	
___ 33. recent reports		___ 33. the doctor's advice	
___ 34. and denials		___ 34. in cap and gown	
___ 35. a pretty stewardess		___ 35. thrift	
___ 36. an eye for an eye		___ 36. insurance dealer	
___ 37. no copilot		___ 37. never any rest	
___ 38. autogiro		___ 38. peace and quiet	
___ 39. a fateful day		___ 39. weather forecaster	
___ 40. with great sorrow		___ 40. courteous taxi driver	

STOP ◆   **STOP ◆**

Time _____   Errors _____   Time _____   Errors _____
The key is on page 188.

List Three ◆ TERMS FROM THE HEALTH SERVICES

The health services are of outstanding importance in the occupational world of today. There is a growing demand for the services of doctors, dentists, and pharmacists, and for the duties performed by nurses, nurses' aids, dietitians, X-ray technicians, physical therapists, and others. The educational requirements are as diverse as the occupations themselves. Professional workers must complete a number of years of specialized training and pass a state licensing examination. On the other hand, some health service occupations are largely without specialized requirements.

A continued rapid expansion of employment in the health fields is expected throughout this decade.[3] Also expected is a growth in interest on the part of the general public in better health for everyone.

Most of the items in List Three are medical terms. None are highly technical, however; all have been selected for their importance to everyone.

[3] *Occupational Outlook Handbook, Career Information for Use in Guidance,* Bulletin No. 1450, U. S. Department of Labor (Washington, D. C.: U. S. Government Printing Office, 1967), pp. 83–130.

WORD	SYLLABLES	PRONUNCIATION
asphyxiate	as phyx′ i ate	as **FIX′** i ate
anesthetic	an′ es thet′ ic	an′ es **THET′** ik
tourniquet	tour′ ni quet	**TOUR′** ni kay or **TOUR′** ni ket
demise	de mise′	de **MIZE′**
therapeutic	ther′ a peu′ tic	ther′ a **PEW′** tik

MEANINGS[4]

asphyxiate	suffocate because of lack of oxygen
anesthetic	something that causes loss of feeling of pain, touch, cold, and so on: *Ether is an anesthetic.*
tourniquet	device for stopping bleeding by compressing a blood vessel; a bandage, for example, tightened by twisting a stick
demise	death
therapeutic	having to do with treatment or cure of an ailment; curative
fatality	accident or happening resulting in death: *Doctors are working to reduce fatality from disease.*
fracture	the breaking of a bone, or, sometimes, a cartilage: in a simple fracture the bone is broken but there is no connecting wound from the break to the skin; in a compound fracture, the bone is broken and in addition there is a wound from the break to the surface.
chronic	continuing a long time: *Rheumatism is sometimes a chronic disease.*
acute	sharp and severe: *A bad tooth often causes acute pain.*
malignant	very harmful, very dangerous, tending or threatening to produce death
antidote	medicine or remedy that acts against a poison; preventive
allergy	unusual sensitiveness to a certain substance. An allergic person may react with violent symptoms in the nose, skin, legs, or eyes when the substance to which he is allergic gets to his body. Some of the substances are ragweed, dog fur, and powder.
epidemic	rapid spread of a disease so that many people have it at the same time
transfusion	transfer of blood from one person to another, or from one animal to another
concussion	injury to the brain or spine caused by a fall, blow, or shock

[4] Not all meanings are given.

malnutrition	poor nourishment or lack of nourishment
contagious	spread by contact: *Scarlet fever is a contagious disease.*
insomnia	sleeplessness; inability to sleep
symptom	change in the normal working of the body that indicates disease, sickness; a sign or indication
post-mortem	after death; examination made after death, autopsy

GENERAL WORDS

sporadic	occurring here and there; occurring now and then
ominous	threatening; unfavorable; sinister: *Ominous threats were made over the phone.*
overt	open to view; obvious; apparent: *The police reported no overt acts of violence.*
covert	secret; hidden; disguised: *Covert glances passed between the two conspirators.*
imminent	about to occur; apt to happen soon: *Dark clouds suggested that a storm was imminent.*
ingenuous	simple, open, frank, sincere: *A great scholar, he was nevertheless as ingenuous as a child.*

Exercise 14 ✦ CHANGING WORD FORMS

DIRECTIONS ✦ Complete each sentence by filling in the blank with the correct word.

1. Change *allergy* to an adjective.

   Some people are _____ to the fur of cats.　　1. ___

2. Change *asphyxiate* to a noun.

   Three of the fire victims died of _____.　　2. ___

3. Exchange *insomnia* for a related noun.

   One who does not sleep is an _____.　　3. ___

4. Change *malnutrition* to an adjective.

   It is possible to eat large quantities of food and still be _____.　　4. ___

5. Change *contagious* to a noun.

   One function of the Health Department is to prevent the spread of

   _____.　　5. ___

6. Think of a noun related to *therapeutic*.

   There is a growing demand today for trained physical _____.   6. ___

7. The word *chronic* comes from a Greek root *chronos*, meaning *time*. Write a word from the same root meaning "a record of events."

   _____   7. ___

8. Change *fatality* to an adjective.

   The number of _____ accidents on the highways is increasing.   8. ___

9. Think of a word related to *insomnia*.

   A person who walks in his sleep is a _____.   9. ___

10. Change *therapeutic* to a noun.

   Occupational _____ often makes it possible for disabled persons to become self-supporting.   10. ___

The key is on page 188.   Number of correct answers ___

Exercise 15 ✦ MATCHING WORDS AND MEANINGS

DIRECTIONS ✦ On the blank beside each key word at the right, place the letter of the best definition at the left. Work from memory.

a) injury to the brain or spine caused by a blow, fall, or shock   demise   1. ___

b) sign or indication of an ailment   epidemic   2. ___

c) remedy to act against a poison   concussion   3. ___

d) abnormal hunger   antidote   4. ___

e) death   symptom   5. ___

f) sleepwalking

g) rapid spread of a disease to many people at the same time

h) X-ray treatment

The key is on page 188.   Number of correct answers ___

Exercise 16 ◆ MATCHING WORDS AND MEANINGS

DIRECTIONS ◆ Proceed according to directions for Exercise 15.

a) frank, sincere, childlike

b) about to occur, threatening

c) reaching a crisis in a short time

d) occurring here and there

e) immature; not ready

f) curative

g) lasting a long time

h) spread by contact

i) very harmful; deadly

sporadic	1.___
therapeutic	2.___
chronic	3.___
contagious	4.___
imminent	5.___

The key is on page 188.

Number of correct answers _____

Exercise 17 ◆ MATCHING WORDS AND MEANINGS

DIRECTIONS ◆ Proceed according to directions for Exercise 15.

a) real; actual; definite

b) subdued; spiritless

c) lawless; immoral

d) greedy; ravenous; eating much

e) truthful

f) timid; shy; lacking in self-confidence

g) not fond of talking

h) concise; using few words in speech

i) easily carried

diffident	1.___
taciturn	2.___
laconic	3.___
voracious	4.___
tangible	5.___

The key is on page 188.

Number of correct answers _____

INTERESTING WORD ORIGINS

investigate   (Latin, *vestigium*, footprint, and *vestigare*, to follow the footprints.) Originally the word had the meaning of tracking down.

ambulance   (Latin, *ambulare*, to walk.) At one time temporary field hospitals were referred to as "walking hospitals."

curfew   In the Middle Ages people were required to cover their fires at a certain time in the evening, the time being announced by the ringing of a bell called the "cover fire." The word curfew comes from two French words meaning "to cover the fire."

Exercise 18 ◆ WORDS OFTEN CONFUSED

DIRECTIONS ◆ Fill in each blank with the most suitable word from the list below.

confidant	biennial	overt
confident	biannual	covert
ingenuous	compliment	imminent
ingenious	complement	eminent

1. The market had its full _____
   of clerks and needed to hire no more at that time.   1. ___

2. The patient was gravely ill; death seemed _____ .   2. ___

3. A sale is _____ if it takes place every six months; it is
   _____ if it occurs every two years.   3. ___

4. The president of the company was close-mouthed; he had just one
   _____ with whom he shared business secrets.   4. ___

5. Probably there is no one who does not treasure a sincere
   _____ from a friend.   5. ___

6. His class work has been good; he feels _____
   he will pass the final examination.   6. ___

7. His death was a great loss to the community; he was _____
   as both a physician and surgeon.   7. ___

8. Occasional inventions are accidental, but most reflect the hard and
   _____ thinking of the inventor.   8. ___

9. The statesman's plan was _____ ;
   it was open to view, public, manifest.   9. ___

10. _____ references to the sale of the building were made
    throughout the conference. There was no attempt to keep the transaction a
    secret.   10. ___

11. Two right angles _____ each other to form a straight
    angle.   11. ___

12. _____ glances passed between the two. They did not
    wish to acknowledge to the group their lifelong friendship.   12. ___

The key is on page 188.   Number of correct answers _____

SPELLING

Chances are that in learning the meanings of the words in your lists, you also learned their spellings. Nevertheless it is important always to have in mind your spelling competence.

Some of the words of your lists are given below. Look at each one quickly. Then cover it, write it, and check. If your spelling was correct and you have no doubts about it, move on to the next word.

If the word requires study, work quickly but effectively. Look at the word as a whole or in large units: *taci turn*, for example, or *thera peutic*. Seek out the hard spots and give them the attention they need. Once again, look at the word as a whole. Then cover it and write it from memory. Check.

Have in mind the goal of *rapid* but *effective* study. Avoid unnecessary letter-by-letter repetition. Avoid also the habit of relying always upon "the next time."

contagious _____ _____ _____

tourniquet _____ _____ _____

concussion _____ _____ _____

therapeutic _____ _____ _____

anesthetic _____ _____ _____

asphyxiate _____ _____ _____

malignant _____ _____ _____

epidemic _____ _____ _____

reminisce _____ _____ _____

taciturn _____ _____ _____

Section Four

Exercise 19 ✦ DISCOVERING WORD MEANINGS
THROUGH CONTEXT CLUES

DIRECTIONS ✦ From each passage try to discover the meaning of the *italicized* word. Then write a brief definition on the blank.

1. When he planned and rehearsed his speeches, they seemed forced and unnatural. His best efforts were always *extemporaneous*.

   _____ 1. ___

2. Perhaps you can arrange for a friend to pay your monthly bills while you are away on your trip. Then you can *reimburse* him when you return.

   _____ 2. ___

3. There were no well known differences in their points of view. It was the general feeling that once they met, the statesmen would *concur* on the matter.

   _____ 3. ___

4. It proved to be a *tortuous* road, winding and twisting like a snake around the trees and rocks of the mountainside.

   _____ 4. ___

5. Six months were to pass between the removal of the council from the old city offices and the completion of the new ones. In the *interim* the meetings were held in the home of one of the members.

   _____ 5. ___

6. Both English and French are used and understood by nearly everyone there. Most of the citizens are *bilingual*.

   _____ 6. ___

7. There was no *aperture* to let air into the cabinet, and the tiny creature soon died of asphyxiation.

   _____ 7. ___

8. Many people disliked his *propaganda*. They found him interesting and forceful, but resented his systematic efforts to spread his beliefs and opinions.

   _____ 8. ___

9. Kirk had a pilot's license and flew his own plane, but Todd preferred boating, fishing, and other *aquatic* sports.

   _____ 9. ___

10. No words passed between them, but their facial expressions reflected *tacit* approval of the plan.

_____ 10. ___

11. Often he was gloomy, downcast, and dejected. Then suddenly his mood would change and he would be genial and *jocund.*

_____ 11. ___

12. There are probably no judges in the local courts who would doubt his *veracity.*

_____ 12. ___

13. Not a single criminal was executed there in the year 1969. A major reason is the growing opposition to *capital* punishment.

_____ 13. ___

14. Nations in financial need should have no worry about the *precipitous* cessation of American aid. Promises have been given that when aid must be reduced, the reductions will be gradual.

_____ 14. ___

15. The fund provides for the prison's few *amenities.* Because of it there are books, pictures, and record players in some of the cells, and there is an elaborate baseball diamond on the recreation field.

_____ 15. ___

The key is on page 189.   Possible score, 15   Your score _____

A NOTE ON CONTEXT CLUES

The meaning of a word in a particular setting may be revealed by examples or contrasts, by descriptive words, or, at times, by definitions. Alertness to such context clues can be of invaluable help in arriving at the meaning independently, without the necessity of turning to the dictionary during the course of casual reading or listening.

But a warning should be issued against overreliance on context clues. They may suggest only a part of the meaning, or only one meaning of several. Whenever a word is to be added to your active vocabulary for regular use in speaking and writing, check your inference with the dictionary.

Exercise 20 ✦ NOTING VARIED MEANINGS OF EVERYDAY WORDS

Many technical terms have only a single meaning. In electrical engineering a special committee has been responsible for the formulation and adoption of new words for the vocabulary of the profession. Constantly watchful, it has been able to establish suitable terms before unsuitable ones gained currency. The result has been described as a "living, growing, flexible, unambiguous vocabulary in which every word has only one meaning and each meaning only one word."

But technical terms make up only a fraction of the words of English. Many other words have appeared casually, at different times and from different sources, and in consequence have a variety of sharply different meanings. A *bill*, for example, can mean a statement of indebtedness, a bank note, a proposed law, a written accusation, a beak, or a poster.

DIRECTIONS ✦ For each word listed below, write three different meanings. Work from memory.

1. block _____
   _____
   _____

2. post _____
   _____
   _____

3. last _____
   _____
   _____

4. flag _____
   _____
   _____

5. draft _____
   _____
   _____

The key is on page 189.   Possible score, 15   Your score _____

currency	cash; coins and paper money that have government backing; legal tender
default	failure to meet interest or principal payments when they are due
annuity	payment to an insured person based upon an annual rate
subsidy	grant-in-aid; often programmed into installments
disbursement	the act of paying out, or money paid out
franchise	a particular privilege granted by the government, as, for example, the right to operate a system of ferryboats
abscond	steal funds and flee while acting in a trusted capacity
commission	a percentage of a sales price paid to a salesman, broker, or agent
tenancy	the occupation or holding of land, quarters, or property of another; state of being a tenant; occupying and paying rent for the property of another
broker	agent, person who buys and sells for others (for example, real estate, stocks, bonds, cotton, grain)

GENERAL WORDS

eloquent	able to express oneself with force and fluency; expressed with grace and force: *He is an able and eloquent official.*
convene	assemble; meet for a purpose; come together: *Congress will convene in Washington in two weeks.*
clientele	customers; patients; followers: *Any good lawyer in the town can expect a large and appreciative clientele.*
tangible	capable of being touched, seen, or felt; actual, real, definite: *He had no tangible proof of his ownership of the car.*
exuberant	overflowing, abundant, lavish: *The athlete was known for his exuberant good humor.*
adamant	unyielding; firm, immovable: *The manager was adamant in his refusal to discuss the petty complaint.*
deteriorate	become or make worse; depreciate; lessen in value: *With rough handling any car may deteriorate in cash value.*
bizarre	odd, fantastic, queer: *At any masquerade party the costumes are apt to be bizarre.*
mendacity	untruthfulness; the habit of lying: *Well known for his mendacity, he had trouble finding employment.*
stability	firmness; permanence; steadfastness; condition of being fixed in position: *At present some of the smaller countries in the Middle East seem to be lacking in stability.*

Exercise 21 ✦ CHANGING WORD FORMS

DIRECTIONS ✦ Fill in the blank with the required word. Reserve the space at the right for scoring.

1. Change *convene* to a noun. The _____ will be in Chicago.   1.___

2. Change *subsidy* to a verb. There is no plan to _____ the private schools of the city.   2.___

3. Change *eloquent* to a noun. He was known far and wide for the wit and _____ of his speeches.   3.___

4. Change *stability* to an adjective. A new business may hesitate to expand unless the government is _____ .   4.___

5. Exchange *franchise* for a negative word meaning "deprive of a franchise or chartered right." _____   5.___

6. Change *disbursement* to a verb meaning "pay out." _____   6.___

7. A person who pays rent to occupy a building is a _____ .   7.___

8. Write an adjective related to *mendacity*. It is not wise to trust the testimony of a _____ person.   8.___

9. Change *annuity* to a related adverb. The Federal Income Tax must be paid _____ .   9.___

10. Change *exuberant* to a noun. Full of good health and good spirits, he is known everywhere for his _____ .   10.___

The key is on page 189.   Number of correct answers _____

Exercise 22 ✦ MATCHING WORDS AND DEFINITIONS

DIRECTIONS ✦ On the blank beside each key word at the right, print the letter of the best definition at the left.

a) government granted right or privilege   currency   1.___
b) one who brings a lawsuit   annuity   2.___
c) untruthfulness
d) firm, steadfastness   franchise   3.___

e) insurance paid on a yearly basis

f) money in everyday use in a country

g) customers of a business or professional person

h) assembly

i) grant-in-aid

mendacity	4. ___
clientele	5. ___

DIRECTIONS ✦ Follow the above instructions with the next list.

a) make firm, dependable, steady

b) annoy, irritate

c) assemble for a purpose

d) celebrate, rejoice

e) worsen

f) aid with a money grant

g) fail to make payments when they are due

h) steal funds and flee while acting in a trusted capacity

i) change positions frequently

convene	1. ___
subsidize	2. ___
stabilize	3. ___
abscond	4. ___
default	5. ___

The key is on page 189.   Possible score, 10   Your score _____

Exercise 23 ✦ DIRECTIVE WORDS USED IN ESSAY EXAMINATION QUESTIONS

Good answers to examination questions depend in part upon a clear understanding of the directive words used in the questions. These are the words like *compare, contrast, trace, explain, justify,* and *contrast;* they indicate the form the answer should take. Knowledge of the subject matter is, of course, essential, but it is largely without value if it is misused in an answer. If you are asked to *compare* two novels, and you merely sketch the plots, you will get little or no credit for your work. If you are asked to *evaluate* the work of a civic group, it is not sufficient merely to list some of the activities. A reply is good only if it answers the question that was asked.

DIRECTIONS ✦ A few of the key words commonly used in essay examination questions are listed below. From this group, select the best term for each question suggested.

compare	describe	explain	outline
contrast	enumerate	illustrate	summarize
define	evaluate	justify	trace

1. In a class in First Aid, the instructor wants the members to give the meaning of the term *shock*. Which term should he use in his question?

_____   1. ___

2. A group of poisonous garden plants has been discussed in a biology class. In an examination, the professor wants the students to name them, one by one. Which term should he use in his question? _____ 2.___

3. In a political science course, some of the students have stated that they favor a bill currently before Congress, while others oppose it. The professor wants each one to take a stand and then show good reasons for his position. What key term should he use in his question? _____ 3.___

4. A recently published novel is strikingly different from an earlier book by the same author. In a class in English literature, the professor wants the students to consider both books and bring out the points of difference. What directive word should he include in his question? _____ 4.___

5. In a First Aid group, the instructor has explained and demonstrated the use of the tourniquet. He wants the members to list the steps briefly. What directive word should be included in his question? _____ 5.___

6. In a business college, a group studying real estate reads a number of articles on the leasing and purchasing of property. The instructor wants the class members to think over these topics and bring into focus the similarities and differences. What term should he use in his question?

_____ 6.___

7. The lecturer in a class in geography wants the students to give a word picture of the Panama Canal. What is its location, its length, its capacity to carry ships? Through what countries does it pass? To get the reply he wants, what term should he incorporate in his question? _____ 7.___

8. The biography of a prominent statesman is published by a little known writer. The professor of a political science group wants the students to read the book and appraise it, bringing out the good and bad features. Which term should he use in his question? _____ 8.___

9. After a series of lectures on patterns of culture, the lecturer wants the group members to bring together the main points in concise form. What term should he stress?_____ 9.___

10. A sentence in an economics text states, "By late spring, 1901, it seemed that prices had reached their peak and were beginning to decline." If the instructor wants the class members to make clear the reasons behind the statement and to give an interpretation, what term should he choose for his question?

_____ 10.___

11. In an atlas, the word *physiography* is used again and again. If it is the purpose of the questioner to get a clear, concise, and authoritative meaning for this word, what term should be used? _____ 11.___

12. A little known country in the Far East comes into sudden prominence in the news. The instructor in a current affairs group wants to make sure that the members are informed about this country. He wants them to describe the progress, development, and historical events from a given point of origin. What term should he include in his question? _____ 12.___

The key is on page 190.   Your score _____

Exercise 24 ✦ SEEING RELATIONSHIPS

DIRECTIONS ✦ Read each set of words and find the one that does not belong with the others. Write its letter on the blank at the right. Work rapidly.

EXAMPLE ✦ a) plane b) car c) airport d) submarine e) train   <u>c</u>

START ✦

1. a) emerald	b) topaz	c) ring	d) opal	e) ruby	1.___
2. a) ant	b) termite	c) bee	d) mosquito	e) earthworm	2.___
3. a) slipper	b) boot	c) shoe	d) smock	e) sandal	3.___
4. a) wealth	b) fury	c) anger	d) hate	e) rage	4.___
5. a) guitar	b) violin	c) piano	d) drummer	e) flute	5.___
6. a) legend	b) story	c) fable	d) tale	e) grammar	6.___
7. a) voyage	b) jaunt	c) trip	d) scenery	e) tour	7.___
8. a) golf	b) croquet	c) jogging	d) tennis	e) baseball	8.___
9. a) tired	b) ill	c) rested	d) blonde	e) refreshed	9.___
10. a) knapsack	b) aviator	c) plumber	d) salesman	e) doctor	10.___
11. a) lapel	b) cuff	c) sleeve	d) wallet	e) button	11.___
12. a) mite	b) pigeon	c) chicken	d) duck	e) robin	12.___
13. a) kennel	b) pigpen	c) corral	d) cage	e) forage	13.___
14. a) muslin	b) khaki	c) nylon	d) postage	e) silk	14.___
15. a) blizzard	b) tornado	c) cyclone	d) tycoon	e) hurricane	15.___
16. a) editor	b) printer	c) title	d) publisher	e) author	16.___
17. a) ancient	b) aged	c) senile	d) ailing	e) venerable	17.___

18. a) papaya	b) cedar	c) quince	d) orange	e) grape	18.___
19. a) sixteen	b) four	c) twelve	d) ten	e) eight	19.___
20. a) employee	b) clerk	c) salary	d) nurse	e) cashier	20.___

STOP ✦

The key is on page 190.   Your score _____

Exercise 25 ✦ SEEING RELATIONSHIPS

DIRECTIONS ✦ Again, find the word in each set that does not belong with the others and write its letter on the blank at the right. Try to work more rapidly this time.

START ✦

1. a) eel	b) seal	c) reel	d) salmon	e) sole	1.___
2. a) swarm	b) bevy	c) flock	d) pack	e) coyote	2.___
3. a) yacht	b) plane	c) canoe	d) dinghy	e) sailboat	3.___
4. a) blunder	b) lie	c) mistake	d) error	e) slip	4.___
5. a) cereal	b) beef	c) market	d) spinach	e) bread	5.___
6. a) view	b) box	c) coffin	d) basket	e) vase	6.___
7. a) prince	b) queen	c) monarch	d) crown	e) king	7.___
8. a) janitor	b) foreigner	c) lawyer	d) tailor	e) broker	8.___
9. a) measles	b) rabies	c) policy	d) cancer	e) influenza	9.___
10. a) lisp	b) stammer	c) stutter	d) drawl	e) limp	10.___
11. a) eraser	b) pen	c) pencil	d) needle	e) typewriter	11.___
12. a) admiral	b) captain	c) seaman	d) proprietor	e) commander	12.___
13. a) eyelash	b) earlobe	c) lawnmower	d) forehead	e) kneecap	13.___
14. a) donate	b) earn	c) bestow	d) contribute	e) bequeath	14.___
15. a) fawn	b) kitten	c) quail	d) antelope	e) cougar	15.___
16. a) almanac	b) perfect	c) correct	d) flawless	e) errorless	16.___
17. a) luggage	b) wristwatch	c) baggage	d) briefcase	e) portfolio	17.___
18. a) rectangle	b) square	c) quadrangle	d) domicile	e) triangle	18.___
19. a) corridor	b) path	c) freezer	d) hallway	e) avenue	19.___
20. a) narrative	b) report	c) tale	d) talker	e) gossip	20.___

STOP ✦

The key is on page 190.   Your score _____

Exercise 26 ✦ WRITING THE REQUIRED WORD

DIRECTIONS ✦ A few common word parts are listed below. Study their meanings. Then fill in the blanks. Use words with word parts included in the list.

inter	between	intersection, interfere
intra, intro	within, on the inside	intramural
re	back, again	repay, renew
super	above, over	supervisor
dicere, dictum	say, tell	diction, dictate
mittere, missum	send	admit, permission
auto	self	automobile
poly	many, much	polygamy

1. between cities or towns _____ 1.___

2. within a state _____ 2.___

3. having to do with many arts or sciences _____ 3.___

4. foretell _____ 4.___

5. man having more than a human man _____ 5.___

6. restore to a good condition _____ 6.___

7. the time between _____ 7.___

8. woven together; mingled _____ 8.___

9. moving or acting of itself _____ 9.___

10. between nations _____ 10.___

11. person who knows several languages _____ 11.___

12. person's name written by himself _____ 12.___

13. turn back _____ 13.___

14. above or beyond what is natural _____ 14.___

15. send back, pay _____ 15.___

The key is on page 190.   Your score _____

DIRECTIONS ◆ Choose the expression closest in meaning to the *italicized* word and print its letter on the blank at the right.

1. *overt* indications of fear

   a) well hidden   c) verbal
   b) possible   d) evident   1.___

2. a well known *antidote*

   a) remedy against a poison   c) pain reliever
   b) slogan   d) ointment   2.___

3. reported the *fatality*

   a) hold-up   c) accident
   b) murder   d) mishap resulting in death   3.___

4. from a *malignant* growth

   a) extremely painful   c) disfiguring
   b) very dangerous   d) harmless   4.___

5. apply a *tourniquet*

   a) device to stop bleeding   c) antiseptic
   b) splint for a broken bone   d) plastic cover   5.___

6. the treatment of a *contagious* disease

   a) fatal   c) spread by contact
   b) lingering, long lasting   d) food-caused   6.___

7. both chronic and *acute* ailments

   a) minor   c) childhood
   b) lasting a long time d) sharp and severe   7.___

8. the storm is now *imminent*

   a) threatening   c) lightening
   b) in progress   d) increasing in violence   8.___

9. no fear he will *asphyxiate*

   a) bleed to death   c) lose consciousness
   b) die for lack of oxygen   d) starve to death   9.___

10. no *tangible* results

    a) harmful   c) immediate

    b) beneficial   d) actual; definite   10.___

11. resulting from *malnutrition*

    a) disorganization   c) poor nourishment

    b) poverty   d) infection   11.___

12. *covert* glances from one to the other

    a) affectionate   c) secret, hidden

    b) understanding   d) threatening   12.___

13. then decide to *convene*

    a) assemble, come together   c) disband for a time

    b) vote on the matter   d) celebrate   13.___

14. no thought of *deterioration*

    a) disbanding   c) abandonment

    b) lessening in value   d) inflation   14.___

15. know something about the *currency*

    a) present conditions   c) legal tender

    b) habits and customs   d) working conditions   15.___

The key is on page 190.   Number of correct answers _____

Exercise 28 ✦ RECALL

DIRECTIONS ✦ On the blank, write the word defined at the left. Work from memory.

1. fail to make payments when they are due   _____   1.___

2. aid with a grant of money   _____   2.___

3. a special privilege granted by the
government   _____   3.___

4. percentage of a sales price paid
to a salesman   _____   4.___

5. curative, having to do with treatment   _____   5.___

6. injury to the brain or spine
caused by a blow, fall, or shock   _____   6.___

7. transfer of blood from one person to another

_____ 7.___

8. occurring here and there or now and then

_____ 8.___

The key is on page 190.   Your score _____

SPELLING

Check your spelling of the words in Exercise 28. If you made any errors, rewrite the words correctly on the blank page below, then study as before to effect the required improvement.

Section Five

DEFINITIONS

One of the best methods of sharpening and refining word knowledge is the practice of framing definitions. A good definition makes clear the meaning of a word and distinguishes it from other, related words.

What, for example, is a columnist? Consider the value of the following definition: "A columnist is a writer." Obviously that definition is unsatisfactory, for under its terms a columnist may be the author of a personal letter.

Consider another definition: "A columnist is a newspaper writer." Here again, the definition fails to note that the columnist uses his own opinions in writing for a special department of a newspaper. A good definition is clear, sharp, and precise.

Read the passage that follows and in your mind formulate a precise definition of the word *tundra*.

The Tundra[1]

For much of the year, the Alaska tundra lies locked in a long and bitter night. The land is covered by darkness and by a cold so intense it seems to hold life suspended.

The tundra lies near the top of the world and is among the world's harshest habitats. Because of the low precipitation, it can be thought of as an Arctic desert. Water is abundant, but it does little for plant life. Below the surface the ground is frozen into a layer of permafrost and water can not penetrate this layer: it stays near the surface to create a waterlogged soil.

Tundra begins where the northern forests end. The northern cone-bearing trees give way to shallow, rooted, woody plants and to grasses and lichens which sprout and grow quickly during the long summer days.

Animal life is of two kinds. There are some creatures that are active only in the summer and those that are active all year long. Both water fowl and mammals constitute a part of the fauna. The scarcity of vegetation and harshness of climate combine to keep most animal populations low. But there are certain curious exceptions. Caribou, for example, adapt well to the conditions, and the lemming population often grows to an incredible size.

[1] Adapted from *Wildlife on the Public Lands*, U. S. Department of the Interior, Bureau of Land Management (Washington, D.C.: U. S. Government Printing Office, 1964).

Exercise 29 ✦ JUDGING THE DEFINITION

DIRECTIONS ✦ Read the four statements that follow. Place an X after the one that best defines the tundra of Alaska. Place an N after any statement that is too narrow, B after one that is too broad, and M after one that includes a misstatement.

1. The Alaska tundra is a great treeless plain of the northern Arctic regions. It consists of a miry soil with a permanently frozen subsoil, but it supports a growth of shallow-rooted, woody plants, grasses, and lichens. Most of the animal populations are small, but caribou and lemmings exist there in large numbers.

   1.____

2. The Alaska tundra can be defined as an Arctic desert. Water is abundant but it remains near the surface to create a waterlogged soil. Below the surface, the ground is frozen into a layer of permafrost.

   2.____

3. The Alaska tundra is a land of darkness and cold during the greater part of the year. It supports two kinds of animals—those that are active only in the summer, and those that are active throughout the year. Caribou and lemmings exist in great numbers.

   3.____

4. The Alaska tundra lies near the top of the world. Water is abundant and it stays near the surface to encourage the growth of cone-bearing trees and plants of many kinds. Caribou and coyotes adapt well to the conditions, and lemmings exist there in great numbers.

   4.____

The key is on page 191.   Your score _____

Exercise 30 ✦ DEFINITION

DIRECTIONS ✦ The term "football stadium" is in common use today. But what, precisely, is a stadium? Try your skill at writing a definition.

The key is on page 191.   Your wording may differ from that in the suggested definition. If you think you are correct, consult a dictionary. Then judge your effort:

Good _____   Fair _____   Poor _____

In your own words, evaluate your effort.

Exercise 31 ✦ FINDING ANTONYMS

DIRECTIONS ✦ Look at the key word at the left. Then, from the group of words at the right, select the one that is opposite in meaning. Write its letter on the blank. Work quickly. You will have one minute.

START ✦

1. jovial	a) thoughtless	b) downcast	c) clever	d) certain	1.___
2. inhale	a) breathe	b) sleep	c) exhale	d) wonder	2.___
3. partial	a) complete	b) surplus	c) prompt	d) delayed	3.___
4. prudent	a) cautious	b) dull	c) unwise	d) kindly	4.___
5. absence	a) presence	b) arrest	c) failure	d) reply	5.___
6. stationary	a) paper	b) mobile	c) rigid	d) fixed	6.___
7. invisible	a) cloudy	b) silent	c) visible	d) marked	7.___
8. immense	a) minute	b) huge	c) vast	d) messy	8.___
9. diverse	a) similar	b) different	c) varied	d) odd	9.___
10. lessen	a) reduce	b) study	c) increase	d) shrink	10.___
11. praise	a) blame	b) honor	c) approve	d) destroy	11.___
12. wrong	a) incorrect	b) right	c) certain	d) faulty	12.___
13. winner	a) athlete	b) bidder	c) runner	d) loser	13.___
14. mirth	a) glee	b) gloom	c) humor	d) fun	14.___
15. poverty	a) misery	b) affluence	c) hunger	d) want	15.___
16. relieve	a) ease	b) assist	c) follow	d) aggravate	16.___
17. boisterous	a) subdued	b) noisy	c) needy	d) fearful	17.___
18. fictitious	a) actual	b) novel	c) skillful	d) funny	18.___
19. plentiful	a) rich	b) popular	c) costly	d) scarce	19.___
20. loss	a) purse	b) money	c) gain	d) regret	20.___

STOP ✦

The key is on page 191.   Possible score, 20   Your score _____

Exercise 32 ◆ FINDING SYNONYMS

DIRECTIONS ◆ Look at the key word at the left. Then, from the group of words at the right, select the one that is nearest in meaning. Write its letter on the blank. Work quickly. You will have one minute.

START ◆

1. abate	a) flood	b) subside	c) intensify	d) increase	1.___
2. novice	a) teacher	b) lawyer	c) beginner	d) namesake	2.___
3. mortify	a) murder	b) shame	c) praise	d) accuse	3.___
4. feign	a) pretend	b) adopt	c) swear	d) sense	4.___
5. parable	a) model	b) problem	c) truth	d) fable	5.___
6. devastate	a) populate	b) destroy	c) inherit	d) bequeath	6.___
7. nefarious	a) indirect	b) complex	c) wicked	d) imported	7.___
8. skeptical	a) bored	b) amused	c) abrupt	d) doubtful	8.___
9. ominous	a) timely	b) illegal	c) threatening	d) sudden	9.___
10. lament	a) complain	b) mourn	c) forget	d) overlook	10.___
11. abject	a) rumored	b) minor	c) hungry	d) wretched	11.___
12. affluent	a) drained	b) rich	c) ignorant	d) selfish	12.___
13. feline	a) cowlike	b) catlike	c) doglike	d) wolflike	13.___
14. desist	a) explain	b) stop	c) repeat	d) continue	14.___
15. delete	a) remove	b) score	c) repay	d) purchase	15.___
16. sparse	a) prickly	b) green	c) sour	d) scanty	16.___
17. ingenious	a) shameful	b) clever	c) illegal	d) hasty	17.___
18. censure	a) agreement	b) advice	c) criticism	d) reminder	18.___
19. ruthless	a) cruel	b) quick	c) untrue	d) thoughtless	19.___
20. ingenuous	a) moody	b) inventive	c) frank	d) timid	20.___

STOP ◆

The key is on page 191.   Possible score, 20   Your score _____

List Five ◆ TERMS RELATED TO THE DRIVER OCCUPATIONS

Most of the terms in this list were selected from a current occupational outlook handbook.[2] Driving jobs offer excellent opportunities today, so the words in the list take on a special importance.

[2] *Occupational Outlook Handbook, Career Information for Use in Guidance,* Bulletin No. 1450, U. S. Department of Labor (Washington, D.C.: U. S. Government Printing Office, 1967), pp. 422–442.

No doubt most of them are familiar. But can you define them? Can you spell them? Can you use them easily and correctly in your speaking and writing?

Make it a point now to add them to your active vocabulary.

WORD	SYLLABLES	PRONUNCIATION
chassis	chas' sis	**SHAS'** ee or **CHAS'** ee
chauffeur	chauf feur	show **FUR'** or **SHOW'** fur
coupe	cou pe'	koo **PAY'**
accelerator	ac cel' er a tor	ak **SELL'** er ay tor
maneuver	ma neu' ver	ma **NEW'** ver

MEANINGS[3]

chassis	the frame, wheels, and machinery of an automobile; the chassis supports the body
carburetor	device for mixing air with gasoline to make an explosive mixture
ignition	system that explodes the fuel inside the cylinders of an engine, controlled by the ignition key on the dashboard
accelerator	device for regulating the flow of gasoline and therefore the speed of the car; the pedal is operated by the right foot
speedometer	instrument to indicate the number of miles per hour the vehicle is traveling
exhaust	means for the used gasoline or steam to escape from the engine
muffler	device for softening the noise from the exhaust
tractor-trailer	the tractor is a short-chassis vehicle which draws the trailer carrying the freight
sedan	closed automobile seating four or more persons
coupe	closed, two-door automobile, usually seating two to five persons
taxicab	automobile for hire with a meter to record the amount to be paid (*Whimsical origin:* The word "taxicab" comes in part from a French word "cabriole," a leap like that of a goat. Before the days of the automobile, the cabriolet was a light, horse-drawn carriage that seemed to bounce on a rough road like a leaping goat.)
freeway	a controlled access highway intended for through traffic, but with a limited number of entrances and exits (also "expressway")
detour	roundabout way; road that is used when a main or direct road can not be traveled
maneuver	operate (a car) with skill and adroitness
ordinance	an authoritative decree; a public ruling or regulation

[3] Not all meanings are given.

lubricate	apply oil or grease; make smooth and slippery; make easy to operate
routeman	person, sometimes known as driver-salesman, who seeks to increase sales and obtain new business by canvassing potential customers. A wholesale routeman provides services to retail establishments; a retail routeman works directly with the public.
vulcanize	repair rubber by using heat and chemicals to fuse a patch
pneumatic	filled with air; worked by air
lading	act of loading; freight
chauffeur	person whose occupation is driving an automobile; one who drives a car

Exercise 33 ✦ ARRIVING AT MEANINGS THROUGH CONTEXT CLUES

DIRECTIONS ✦ Read each statement and try to arrive at the meaning of the *italicized* word. Then write the meaning on the blank.

1. The scientists estimated that no more than 4,000 whales should be harvested during the year, yet more than three times that number were killed. Why was this horror *condoned?*

   _____   1.___

2. The ticket of the *spectator* allows him only to watch the football game. It does not give him permission to walk on the playing field.

   _____   2.___

3. Acts One and Two end with an *injunction* given to the guards: "If anyone makes a move, shoot."

   _____   3.___

4. The bull stopped as if he felt that his hour had come. Then he staggered and fell. After a finishing stroke from the matador, the bull *expired.*

   _____   4.___

5. The way to control behavior is to reward what is "good" and punish what is "bad." No doubt three out of four readers would *concur* with this concept.

   _____   5.___

6. The critics were in sharp disagreement. Some blamed the manager for his waste and extravagance; others deplored his *parsimony.*

   _____   6.___

7. The protest movement is following the normal pattern. It is not *waning* with the first signs of progress, but getting bolder and more demanding.

_____   7.___

8. His *sojourn* was a brief one, yet he had the opportunity to meet many Englishmen and visit many English homes.

_____   8.___

9. His job is no *sinecure*. He works long hours and receives little pay.

_____   9.___

10. After jet planes drained the profits from its once *lucrative* passenger trade, the company sold its great vessels to investors who hoped to turn them into dockside attractions.

_____   10.___

11. Despite the surprisingly free intellectual climate there, one subject has long remained *taboo*—public speculation about the retirement of the aging president.

_____   11.___

12. The editor expressed the widespread popular indignation at the crime. "How many thefts, arsons, robberies and other crimes have been committed," he asked, "and where are the *perpetrators?*"

_____   12.___

13. The athlete would have it no other way. "I'm happy being five feet nine. I don't think I would like it if I grew tall. Besides," he said, "there are advantages in being a *mite* among monsters."

_____   13.___

14. The heritage of American life is remarkable for a certain vagueness of outline. There is no point at which the law is sharply and definitely supreme; certain rights of citizens always take *precedence*.

_____   14.___

15. Immigration has altered American life. In enriching the American vocabulary, it has been a major force in establishing the "American language" which years ago *diverged* greatly from the mother tongue as spoken in Britain.

_____   15.___

The key is on page 191.   Your score _____

WHIMSICAL WORD ORIGINS

salary   (Originally salt money.) The Roman soldier, as part of his pay, drew a special allowance for the purchase of salt, which was not as easy to obtain in ancient times as it is today. The allowance for salt was called "salarium," and this was later taken into English as salary.[4]

humble   (Literally, on the ground.) *Humus* in Latin means "earth," "ground," and *humilis* means "on the ground." A related word, *humiliate* means "to put on the ground," hence "to humble."

Exercise 34 ◆ SEEING THE MEANINGS OF WORD PARTS

DIRECTIONS ◆ Listed below are ten common word parts. Study their meanings, then explore the everyday words that follow. On the blank at the right, print the letter that identifies the best meaning.

ab-	away, from	abstract
con-, col-	together, with	congregate
fore-	in front of (position, time)	forecast
-hood	state of, condition of	statehood
mal-	wrong, ill, bad	malignant
manus	hand	manual
portare	to carry	porter
semi-, hemi-	half, or partially	semicircle
sentire, sensum	to feel	sense
-temp-	time	temporary

1. The gift was a *portable* typewriter.

     a) electric   c) easily carried

     b) made in this country   d) modern   1.___

2. The writers were *contemporaries*.

     a) school friends   c) authorities in their fields

     b) rivals   d) persons belonging to the same period of time   2.___

3. There was no evidence that the animals were *maltreated*.

     a) abused   c) vaccinated

     b) stolen   d) dangerous   3.___

4. Some people *abhor* snakes.

     a) collect   c) set traps for

     b) shrink away from in horror   d) capture and skin   4.___

[4] *Picturesque Word Origins* (Springfield, Mass.: G. and C. Merriam Company, 1933), pp. 68, 105.

5. The wallet had been *manufactured* abroad.

   a) designed
   b) purchased
   c) made by hand (or machine)
   d) discovered

   5.___

6. Black clouds are sometimes *forerunners* of a storm.

   a) causes
   b) warnings of things to come
   c) side effects
   d) elements

   6.___

7. Checks are sent out *semiannually*.

   a) twice a year
   b) every two years
   c) yearly
   d) frequently

   7.___

8. *Childhood* should be a time of freedom from lasting fears.

   a) time of being a child
   b) state of being afraid
   c) condition of terror
   d) self-assurance

   8.___

9. The brothers will *collaborate* on the work.

   a) decide
   b) agree
   c) act jointly
   d) consult experts

   9.___

10. The path led them through a *malodorous* swamp.

    a) dark, ominous
    b) smelling bad
    c) hot, murky
    d) insect infested

    10.___

11. Some people seem *insensitive* to changes in temperature.

    a) unfeeling
    b) alert
    c) callous
    d) adapted

    11.___

12. Finally the decision was made to *deport* him.

    a) arrest
    b) send out (of the country)
    c) vindicate
    d) accept

    12.___

13. They felt that the apartment would serve them *temporarily*.

    a) adequately
    b) excellently
    c) only poorly
    d) for the time

    13.___

14. Many a book includes a *foreword*.

    a) preface
    b) appendix
    c) glossary
    d) table of contents

    14.___

15. They feared the child had been *abducted*.

    a) injured
    b) poisoned
    c) carried away
    d) terrified

    15.___

The key is on page 191.

Number of correct answers _____

Exercise 35 ◆ SPEED OF INTERPRETATION

DIRECTIONS ◆ Place an X beside each item that includes a verb denoting action or movement. Work rapidly. Keep a time record.

EXAMPLE ◆ ___ an odd question

<u>X</u> to cut taxes

START ◆

___ 1. and many others
___ 2. the newer way
___ 3. shook his head
___ 4. to open the window
___ 5. now and then
___ 6. drove the car
___ 7. today
___ 8. in a restaurant
___ 9. seat the guests
___10. a sick child
___11. charming silhouette
___12. unlettered
___13. a new suit
___14. he backed away
___15. deliver the groceries
___16. then write the letter
___17. cross the street
___18. six months ago
___19. a single rule
___20. the lonely perch
___21. arrest the offenders
___22. fact and fiction
___23. then fell from the tree
___24. selected a name
___25. in the bank
___26. with the others
___27. to purchase the plane
___28. large and friendly
___29. last week
___30. to buy food
___31. and then returned
___32. to break the window
___33. Sunday
___34. his birthday
___35. a baseball
___36. catch the ball
___37. like a game of golf
___38. a mixed lot
___39. in height
___40. wreck the truck

STOP ◆

START ◆

___ 1. the next four films
___ 2. each drop of blood
___ 3. with some tension
___ 4. to visit his friend
___ 5. repair the highway
___ 6. half an hour
___ 7. during the holiday
___ 8. a curt response
___ 9. at the hotel
___10. bit by bit
___11. bake the apples
___12. sow the lawn seed
___13. write a check
___14. a supply ship
___15. they fed the horse
___16. sink or swim
___17. trouble ahead
___18. remove the shoes
___19. a brief rest
___20. Wednesday
___21. climbed the ladder
___22. occasionally
___23. October
___24. wounded a friend
___25. sat down
___26. never
___27. one by one
___28. a warm blanket
___29. covered the child
___30. circulation of the blood
___31. the drawing room
___32. school day
___33. wrote the answer
___34. answered the question
___35. finally
___36. beyond repair
___37. justice
___38. swat the fly
___39. move the wheelbarrow
___40. open the letter

STOP ◆

Time _____ Errors _____

Time _____ Errors _____

The key is on page 192.

Exercise 36 ◆ SPEED OF INTERPRETATION

DIRECTIONS ◆ Place an X before each group of words that mentions anything that is always *entirely animal* in its original form.

EXAMPLE ◆ ____ for the computer

____ X ____ a human earlobe

START ◆

____ 1. by and large
____ 2. a running deer
____ 3. nor steal a child
____ 4. assist a therapist
____ 5. telephone poles
____ 6. colony of ants
____ 7. this area
____ 8. thousands of years
____ 9. just a cyclone
____10. or a tornado
____11. temper tantrum
____12. nurse's aid
____13. registered nurse
____14. routeman
____15. chassis
____16. carburetor
____17. exhaust
____18. temperatures
____19. for the bank teller
____20. or the stenographer
____21. the first spring rain
____22. a loose joint
____23. call a dentist
____24. cool and clear
____25. in the evening
____26. ants and termites
____27. domestic animals
____28. three per acre
____29. Wednesday
____30. counsel
____31. from a counselor
____32. mortar and brick
____33. nails and hammers
____34. like a queen bee
____35. over the radio
____36. good announcer
____37. snore loudly
____38. only a young robin
____39. dime and a nickel
____40. subsidy

STOP ◆

START ◆

____ 1. the new ambassador
____ 2. a misdemeanor
____ 3. told the tenant
____ 4. in the forest
____ 5. rainbow in the sky
____ 6. the family dog
____ 7. rabbits are rodents
____ 8. a new client
____ 9. for the proprietor
____10. no stability
____11. tangible evidence
____12. advise an anesthetic
____13. visit the consul
____14. pay the debt
____15. or be a defaulter
____16. as you wish
____17. nail polish
____18. boots and shoes
____19. few foreign traders
____20. a long, loose robe
____21. contraband
____22. one's adversary
____23. the front porch
____24. without a dietitian
____25. pot of gold
____26. below the surface
____27. and no chauffeur
____28. not a competitor
____29. for quite a while
____30. by an arsonist
____31. the point of a gun
____32. frightening
____33. loud and clear
____34. dark and quiet
____35. litter of puppies
____36. two swine
____37. moths and butterflies
____38. his beneficiary
____39. a new patrolman
____40. an able speaker

STOP ◆

Time _____ Errors _____
The key is on p. 192.

Time _____ Errors _____

DIRECTIONS ◆ Read the brief definition at the left, then fill in the blank with the required word. Give careful attention to the spelling. Work from memory.

1. word that means the opposite of another word   _____   1. ___

2. suffocate because of lack of oxygen   _____   2. ___

3. flesh-eating   _____   3. ___

4. having to do with the treatment or curing of a disease; curative   _____   4. ___

5. privilege granted by a government   _____   5. ___

6. lying; untruthfulness   _____   6. ___

7. pay based on a percentage of the amount of business done   _____   7. ___

8. speaking little; not fond of talking   _____   8. ___

9. failure to make payment when the payment is due   _____   9. ___

10. unusual sensitiveness to a particular substance, such as cat fur   _____   10. ___

11. injury to brain or spine caused by a sudden, violent blow, fall, or shock   _____   11. ___

12. frank, sincere, childlike   _____   12. ___

13. apprentice; beginner   _____   13. ___

14. foreign; not native; strange   _____   14. ___

15. person who buys and sells real estate, insurance, goods, and so on, for others   _____   15. ___

16. grant-in-aid, often paid out in installments   _____   16. ___

17. medicine or remedy that counteracts a poison   _____   17. ___

18. shy; lacking in self-confidence   _____   18. ___

19. area where plant or animal lives   _____   19. ___

20. unyielding; firm; immovable   _____   20. ___

21. very dangerous; threatening to cause death   _____   21. ___

22. group of customers; group of persons for whom a lawyer acts   _____   22. ___

23. injury or other happening resulting in death   _____ 23.___

24. person trusted with one's secrets or private affairs   _____ 24.___

25. procession of persons riding on horseback   _____ 25.___

26. something that causes the loss of feeling for pain, heat, touch   _____ 26.___

27. real, actual, capable of being touched or felt   _____ 27.___

28. word meaning the same or nearly the same as another   _____ 28.___

29. secret; hidden, disguised   _____ 29.___

30. docile; easily managed   _____ 30.___

The key is on page 192.   Possible score, 60   Your score _____

Scoring: Give yourself one point if you knew the word that was required. Give yourself a second point if you spelled it correctly. If any answer differs from the one in the key, check with the dictionary.

Give special attention to the correction of any words you may have misspelled. Work from the list in the key on page 192.

Look over the word as a whole, or in large units. Then concentrate on the hard spots. Work for quick mastery. As soon as you think you know the spelling, write it out from memory. Then check immediately. If your spelling was correct and you entertain no doubts about it, go on to the next word needing attention.

If you made any error, repeat the study process. Look at the word, check the hard spots, then write from memory. Repeat the process as often as necessary, but keep each exposure period brief. Work to improve your speed of learning.

Section Six

Insurance is a multibillion dollar business which employs more people than such great industries as automobile and aircraft manufacturing, banking, or hotels. It offers opportunities both to young people just out of college or high school and to experienced workers.

Insurance companies sell policies which provide not only basic life insurance protection, but several other kinds of protection as well. Some policyholders receive an income when they reach retirement age, or if they are disabled. Others are provided with health and accident insurance. There are property and liability policies, and group policies issued to employers for the benefit of their employees.

List Six is made up of introductory terms in the field.

List Six ◆ INSURANCE TERMS

policy	certificate of insurance; written insurance contract
premium	money paid for insurance
casualty	accident (casualty insurance is protection against one's legal liability for injury to or death of another); type of insurance against loss from an accident
indemnity	security against loss; payment for damage or loss or expense incurred
arson	crime of intentionally setting fire to a building or other property
dividend	share of the profits made by the insurance company and paid to the policy holder
solicit	ask for trade or business
mutual	having to do with a company in which the policyholders are, in effect, company members and share the profits (in the form of dividends)
salesworker	broker or agent whose work is selling insurance
underwriter	person in the insurance business signing the policy and thus accepting the risk against loss
actuary	person who figures risks, rates, and premiums for an insurance company
beneficiary	person who receives money or property from an insurance company
accountant	person who takes care of company records and financial problems relating to premiums, investments, payments, and so on
warranty	guarantee of title or contract; pledge
claims adjuster	employee who settles claims made against his company

List Seven ✦ GENERAL WORDS

acquit	declare not guilty: *If the members of a jury find a man innocent, they acquit him.*
evoke	call forth; bring out: *The bizarre clothing of the new salesman evoked much criticism.*
migrant	person, animal, bird, or plant that moves from one place to settle in another: *Many birds are migrants.*
vigilant	watchful; alert: *The prison guards remained vigilant throughout the night.*
potent	powerful: *The drug was too potent to be tested on humans.*
nocturnal	of the night; active at night: *The owl is a nocturnal creature.*
authentic	genuine, reliable, sure: *How does the expert tell when the signature on a check is authentic?*
dogmatic	positive; asserting opinions as if by the highest authority: *The dogmatic statement is often asserted without proof.*
myriad	very large number: *Myriads of insects thrive in the jungles there.*
enigma	puzzle: *To most of the audience, the scientist seemed to speak in enigmas.*

Exercise 38 ✦ CHANGING WORD FORMS

DIRECTIONS ✦ Fill in the blank with the required word.

1. Change *acquit* to a noun. Everyone believed the man innocent; no one was

   surprised at his _____   1.___

2. Exchange *evoke* for a related word meaning "take back, cancel, withdraw."

   If he fails to pass the examination the examiner will _____
   his license.   2.___

3. Change *migrant* to a verb. They plan to _____
   to England.   3.___

4. Change *vigilant* to a noun. Constant _____ is
   essential if one is to avoid accidents in driving.   4.___

5. Change *enigma* to an adjective. His expression was _____ ;
   no one was certain of his opinion on the matter.   5.___

6. Change *arson* to a related noun form. One who intentionally sets a building

   on fire is an _____ .   6.___

7. Change *solicit* to a noun. The company hired a _____
to go from office to office trying to build up trade.   7.___

8. The word *nocturnal* means "by night" or "of the night." Write the adjective
that means "of or belonging to the day." _____   8.___

9. Change *potent* to a noun meaning "ruler, person having great power."

_____   9.___

10. Change the word *council* for a homonym meaning "one who gives advice."

_____   10.___

11. Change *statue* for a similar word meaning "law." _____ 11.___

12. Change *desert* for a similar word meaning a "part of a meal."

_____   12.___

The key is on page 192.   Possible score, 12   Your score _____

Exercise 39 ✦ FRAMING A DEFINITION

DIRECTIONS ✦ Read the following passage to get a clear, concise idea of the term *rationalization*. Think first of the general meaning, then set up limits.

Rationalization[1]

Rationalization is the process by which we fool ourselves with our own alibis when
we encounter failure, frustration, or threats to our self-esteem. It helps us to replace
the real reasons with ego-sparing reasons to explain why we cannot solve a problem.

Perhaps the best known defense by rationalization is the *sour grapes* reaction, from
the story of the frustrated fox who justified his failure to obtain the grapes by calling
them sour. In this way he converted the *unattainable* into the *undesirable*. This
same mechanism is illustrated in the behavior of a young man who misses out on
a job he wanted very much and tried very hard to get. When he learns that someone
else has been hired, he begins to belittle the job in order to defend himself against
his feelings of failure. He insists that he really did not want the job in the first
place—that it did not pay enough, that it required too much work.

The reverse of the sour-grapes mechanism is what is sometimes called the *sweet
lemon* reaction. Instead of trying to convince himself and others that he did not
really want what he failed to get, someone using this mechanism is concerned with
convincing himself that he likes what he has to put up with. This reaction is
illustrated by those who insist that life suits them fine just the way it is, even though
they may be living in squalor. Similarly, the man who is never promoted, whose
job seems to be leading nowhere, is rationalizing in this manner when he says he
likes what he is doing and does not want to do anything else.

[1] G. F. Lehner and E. Kube, *The Dynamics of Personal Adjustment*, 2nd ed. (Englewood Cliffs, N J.:
Prentice-Hall, Inc., 1964), pp. 126–127.

Write your summary-definition in the space below. Confine it to a single short paragraph.

The key is on page 192.   Your rating _____

WORD USAGE

Effectiveness in speaking and writing depends in important measure upon a broad knowledge of words and their meanings. It also depends upon a studious concern for word usage and a continuing interest in always selecting the best word available.

Exercise 40 ◆ WORD USAGE

DIRECTIONS ◆ The words listed below name groups of people moving along together. Read each definition at the left, then fill in the blank.

cavalcade	file	parade	procession
cortege	pageant	pilgrimage	promenade

1. any orderly movement forward   _____ 1. ___

2. a walk for pleasure or for show, as at Easter   _____ 2. ___

3. line of people moving one behind another   _____ 3. ___

4. group of people moving along together on
   horseback or in carriages   _____ 4. ___

5. elaborate spectacle, often with floats, or
   a procession of people in costume   _____ 5. ___

6. ceremonial march of troops for a high officer   _____ 6. ___

7. company of tourists, merchants, or others
   traveling together to a shrine   _____ 7. ___

8. train of attendants or followers, as at a
   funeral   _____ 8. ___

The key is on page 193.   Your score _____

Exercise 41 ✦ WORD USAGE

DIRECTIONS ✦ This time supply the missing word without a guide list. Each item defines a kind of speaking or talking. Fill in the blank with a single verb.

1. ask in order to find out   _____ 1.___

2. give a planned talk on a chosen subject   _____ 2.___

3. argue about in a public meeting   _____ 3.___

4. speak wildly, violently, noisily   _____ 4.___

5. repeat, say over, as in learning a lesson   _____ 5.___

6. talk informally with someone; exchange ideas _____ 6.___

7. talk rapidly, steadily, and foolishly   _____ 7.___

8. give a spoken reply   _____ 8.___

The key is on page 193.   Your score _____

Exercise 42 ✦ WORD USAGE

DIRECTIONS ✦ The expressions at the left name different kinds of winds and windstorms. On the blank, write the word defined.

1. soft, gentle breeze   _____ 1.___

2. violent windstorm with great cold and snow   _____ 2.___

3. sudden sharp rush of wind   _____ 3.___

4. violent and destructive funnel of wind
   extending down from dark clouds   _____ 4.___

5. strong, continuing wind   _____ 5.___

6. storm with wind and rain, the wind blowing
   70 to 100 miles per hour   _____ 6.___

The key is on page 193.   Your score _____

Exercise 43 ✦ FRAMING A DEFINITION

DIRECTIONS ✦ On the blank, write a brief definition for the word at the left.

1. shanty _____ 1.___

2. mansion _____ 2.___

3. cottage _____ 3.___

4. penthouse _____ 4.___

The key is on page 193.   Your score _____

Exercise 44 ✦ COMPLETING ANALOGIES

DIRECTIONS ✦ Below is a list of incomplete analogies. With each item, decide on the nature of the relationship; then complete the analogy by writing in the missing word.

EXAMPLE ✦ books : library : : words : _____dictionary_____

amateur	defeated	glacier	provender
banquet	deft	liability	sedan
carnivore	esthetic	malicious	skeptic
contralto	flooded	mathematics	vehicle
covey	fracture	preface	vocation

1. obscure : distinct : : victorious : _____   1.___

2. fire : gutted : : water : _____   2.___

3. school : whales : : _____ : quail   3.___

4. soprano : _____ : : tenor : bass   4.___

5. expert : _____ : : fiction : actuality   5.___

6. fire : burn : : fall : _____   6.___

7. herbivore : cow : : _____ : lion   7.___

8. geography : oceanography : : _____ : trigonometry   8.___

9. disaster : earthquake : : _____ : teaching   9.___

10. _____ : conclusion : : ante-bellum : post-bellum   10.___

11. _____ : fodder : : fruits : papaya   11.___

12. ice : _____ : : water : river   12.___

13. asset : intelligence : : _____ : stupidity   13.___

14. benevolent : _____ : : deft : clumsy   14.___

15. car : _____ : : tool : hammer   15.___

16. snack : _____ : : cottage : mansion   16.___

The key is on page 193.   Your score _____

Exercise 45 ✦ MAKING USE OF PREFIX KNOWLEDGE

DIRECTIONS ✦ Listed below are a few common prefixes. Some are already familiar. Look at the meanings, then explore the everyday words that follow. On the blank at the right print the letter which identifies the best meaning.

ante-	before
anti-	against
bene-	well, good
circum-	around
inter-	between, among, together
intra-	within, inside, on the inside
mal-	wrong, ill, bad, badly, poorly
super-	above, over, exceedingly

1. for the *maltreatment* of the child

   a) starvation   c) health care
   b) discipline   d) abuse   1.____

2. an *intercity* bus driver

   a) experienced   c) between cities
   b) rural   d) government owned   2.____

3. to *supervise* the apprentices

   a) oversee; direct   c) furnish
   b) examine   d) encourage   3.____

4. travel on *intrastate* business

   a) routine   c) within the state
   b) charitable   d) among the states   4.____

5. proved to be a *benefactor*

   a) one who has given kindly help   c) social butterfly
   b) gossip   d) man of wealth   5.____

6. *antipathy* for a relative

   a) strong dislike   c) fondness
   b) respect   d) bequest   6.____

7. to *circumscribe* an area on the map

   a) locate   c) color
   b) draw a line around d) search for   7.____

8. an *ante-bellum* story

   a) military   c) factual

   b) improbable   d) before the war   8.___

9. with *superhuman* effort

   a) animal   c) above what is human

   b) unbelievable   d) substandard   9.___

10. of little *benefit* to an athlete

   a) advantage   c) interest

   b) harm   d) encouragement   10.___

11. stories of *supernatural* creatures

   a) imaginary   c) of the distant past

   b) subhuman   d) above what is natural   11.___

12. *interplanetary* travel

   a) space   c) planned for the future

   b) between planets   d) occurring now and then   12.___

13. a *malicious* disposition

   a) spiteful   c) cheery

   b) lazy   d) kindly   13.___

14. to prescribe an *antidote*

   a) sedative   c) tonic

   b) pain killer   d) remedy to counteract a   14.___
                                 poison

15. *antedating* the Civil War

   a) starting   c) happening before

   b) occurring at the same time d) following   15.___

The key is on page 193.   Your score _____

Exercise 46 ✦ CHOOSING THE BETTER WORD

DIRECTIONS ✦ On the blank, write the word of your choice.

1. New members will be selected in April to serve on the city *counsel/council.*

_____   1.___

2. Thomas A. Edison was *eminent/imminent* both as electrician and inventor.

$\underline{\hspace{7cm}}$ 2.___

3. To slow down the speed of the car you are driving, apply the *brake/break*.

$\underline{\hspace{7cm}}$ 3.___

4. A large city hospital requires the services of a large *corps/corpse* of trained

workers $\underline{\hspace{5cm}}$ 4.___

5. Each night the traveler wrote down some of his impressions in his *dairy/diary*.

$\underline{\hspace{7cm}}$ 5.___

6. The teacher began the day by checking attendance; as a rule she called the

roll/role out loud. $\underline{\hspace{4cm}}$ 6.___

7. There were *covert/overt* references to the merger throughout the meeting. No

one attempted to keep the matter secret. $\underline{\hspace{3cm}}$ 7.___

8. When a celebration takes place regularly every second year, it becomes a

biannual/biennial affair. $\underline{\hspace{3.5cm}}$ 8.___

9. Boston is the *principal/principle* city of Massachusetts.

$\underline{\hspace{7cm}}$ 9.___

10. The chef was famous for his apple pie. Everyone wanted a copy of his

recipe/receipt. $\underline{\hspace{4cm}}$ 10.___

11. The street there was narrow and winding; a city *ordnance/ordinance* forbade

parking there. $\underline{\hspace{4cm}}$ 11.___

12. Recent grants of money are expected to *effect/affect* great changes in the

administration of the college. $\underline{\hspace{3cm}}$ 12.___

13. The eyes and ears are *sensual/sensory* organs. $\underline{\hspace{2.5cm}}$ 13.___

14. Deep mud made the road *impossible/impassable;* the cars were forced to turn

back. $\underline{\hspace{4.5cm}}$ 14.___

15. He wrote so rapidly that his scribble was *illegible/eligible*.

$\underline{\hspace{7cm}}$ 15.___

16. Precinct workers will *canvas/canvass* the area in an effort to "get out the vote." _____ 16.___

17. After organizing and studying the material he felt *confidant/confident* he would pass the examination. _____ 17.___

18. The astronaut was a man of greater than average *statute/stature*.

_____ 18.___

19. Proper names should begin with *capitol/capital* letters.

_____ 19.___

20. A stone is an *inept/inert* mass of matter. _____ 20.___

21. The hillside took on a greenish *hew/hue*. _____ 21.___

22. Clever and inventive, he was known far and wide as an *ingenuous/ingenious* man. _____ 22.___

23. At the wedding the bride's cousins served as her *attendance/attendants*.

_____ 23.___

24. A *hoard/horde* of mosquitoes descended upon the picnic party.

_____ 24.___

25. Cancer is a highly dangerous *decease/disease*. _____ 25.___

The key is on page 194. Your score _____

Exercise 47 ✦ SPOTTING SUPERFLUOUS WORDS

DIRECTIONS ✦ Some of the items in this exercise include words that are not needed. Identify these items with X's and cross out the superfluous words.

___ 1. a widow woman

___ 2. the daily newspaper

___ 3. at nine A.M. in the morning

___ 4. differences of opinion

___ 5. predict the outcome ahead of time

___ 6. annual awards made once a year

___ 7. visitors from Europe

___ 8. the idea still persists

____ 9. the submarine caves under the water

____10. from dusk to dawn

____11. resembling the puzzling enigmas of the past

____12. entering the stadium

____13. six survivors

____14. interurban flights between cities

____15. prepaid in advance

____16. a scholarly work

____17. self-centered egotism

____18. the present incumbent on the council

____19. the same materials

____20. currently on exhibit at the present time

____21. no nonsense

____22. unforeseen difficulties

____23. the end of an era

____24. an upward ascent

____25. post-mortem examination made after death

The key is on page 194.   Your score _____

Exercise 48 ◆ THE MEANINGS OF COMMON WORD PARTS

DIRECTIONS ◆ Write the meaning of the word part on the blank.

1. The *tele* in *telephone* and *telegraph* means _____ 1.___

2. The *im* in *impatient* means _____ 2.___

3. The *ify* in *purify* means _____ 3.___

4. The *itis* in *appendicitis* means _____ 4.___

5. The *pre* in *prepaid* means _____ 5.___

6. The *trans* in *transport* means _____ 6.___

7. The *sub* in *submerge* means _____ 7.___

8. The *ology* in *geology* means _____ 8.___

9. The *il* in *illegal* means _____ 9.___

10. The *con* in *converse* means _____ 10.___

The key is on page 194.   Your score _____

DIRECTIONS ◆ On the blank beside each key word at the right, print the letter of the best definition to be found in the column at the left. Work from memory.

Part A

a) the holding of land, quarters, or property of another, in return for the payment of rent

b) the grant of a special privilege by the government

c) a grant-in-aid; financial grant

d) legal tender; cash or money

e) payment to an insured person based on an annual rate

f) an assembly for business talks

g) salesman, agent

h) money paid out

broker   1. ___

annuity   2. ___

tenancy   3. ___

franchise   4. ___

subsidy   5. ___

Part B

a) means for used steam or gasoline to escape from an engine

b) panel in the front of an automobile containing instruments and gauges

c) metal covering over the engine of an automobile

d) frame, wheels, and machinery of an automobile

e) instrument to indicate the number of miles per hour the vehicle is traveling

f) device for mixing air with gasoline to make an explosive mixture

g) sheet of glass to keep off the wind

h) device for regulating the flow of gasoline and therefore the speed of the car

accelerator   1. ___

carburetor   2. ___

chassis   3. ___

exhaust   4. ___

speedometer   5. ___

Part C

a) medicine or remedy that acts against a poison

b) happening resulting in death

c) inability to sleep

d) the breaking of a bone or, sometimes, a cartilage

e) suffocation from lack of oxygen

f) death

g) serious illness threatening death

h) something that causes loss of feeling for pain, cold, touch, and so on

demise   1. ___

fracture   2. ___

asphyxiation   3. ___

antidote   4. ___

fatality   5. ___

a) easily managed or controlled

b) broken down by age

c) flesh-eating

d) uncertain; doubtful

e) shy; lacking in self-confidence

f) inclined to doubt

g) occurring here and there

h) spread by contact

skeptical	1.___
diffident	2.___
tractable	3.___
carnivorous	4.___
sporadic	5.___

Part E

a) think about or talk over events of the past

b) clear of suspicion or charge of wrongdoing

c) waste; lavish

d) keep within limits

e) purloin funds and flee while acting in a trusted capacity

f) make or become worse

g) assemble; meet for a purpose

h) operate (a car) with skill and adroitness

squander	1.___
abscond	2.___
deteriorate	3.___
reminisce	4.___
vindicate	5.___

Part F

a) person signing an insurance policy and thus accepting the risk against loss

b) salesman

c) person who receives money or property from an insurance policy

d) statistical expert who figures risks, rates, and premiums for an insurance company

e) employee who settles claims against a company

f) criminal who sets fires to property

g) person who records changes in policies

h) insurance instructor

claims adjuster	1.___
beneficiary	2.___
underwriter	3.___
actuary	4.___
broker	5.___

The key is on page 194.   Possible score, 30   Your score _____

MIDWAY APPRAISAL OF YOUR PROGRESS

In Section One you directed your attention to certain key factors related to your word competence. You wrote out a statement of the ways in which you wished to improve.

At this point consider the progress you have made, particularly in your independent work. What can you say of your alertness to new words with special significance in the field of your specialization, in the courses you are taking, and in your day-by-day life? What of your habits of word attack and your concern for effective usage?

Where do you see improvement? Where do you need to put forth special effort? Write out a brief statement.

Section Seven

Government service provides jobs for millions of workers each year.[1] Studies indicate that the demand for Federal, State, and local government workers will increase rapidly throughout the current decade.[2] Widely varied activities will require a diversified work force with many different levels of education, training, and skills, and will provide opportunities both at home and abroad.

The words in List Eight should be familiar to people who look forward to careers in government service. But they should also be known by others—by oral hygienists, commercial artists, automobile mechanics, airplane dispatchers, insurance brokers, miners, and bank tellers, to name just a few. The words are of general importance.

List Eight ✦ TERMS OF IMPORTANCE IN THE GOVERNMENT SERVICES

DIRECTIONS ✦ Read these words aloud. Make sure you can pronounce them.

WORD	SYLLABLES	PRONUNCIATION
cartographer	car tog' ra pher	kar **TOG'** ra fer
maintenance	main' te nance	**MAIN'** te nans
statistician	stat is ti' cian	stat is **TI'** shen
visa	vi' sa	**VEE'** za

MEANINGS[3]

cartographer	maker of maps or charts
maintenance	keeping up, carrying on, supporting: *Any government must collect taxes to take care of its maintenance obligations.*

[1] *Occupational Outlook Handbook, Career Information for Use in Guidance*, Bulletin No. 1450, U. S. Department of Labor (Washington, D. C.: U. S. Government Printing Office, 1967), p. 808.

[2] *Time*, February 15, 1971, p. 70.

[3] Not all meanings are given.

statistician	one who collects and studies facts (for example, about the weather, business, or people), then classifies the information systematically
rehabilitation	restoration to former standing, or to a good condition
visa	official signature on a passport or other document showing that it has been approved
alien	foreigner; person who is not a citizen of the country in which he lives or visits
ambassador	highest ranking representative sent by one government to another
consul	official appointed by his government to live in a foreign country and look after the business interests of his country there, and protect the citizens of his country
census	numbering of the population; official count to find the age, sex, occupation, and other traits of each individual
caucus	meeting of the members or leaders of a political party to make plans, choose candidates, and decide how to vote
disfranchise	take away the rights of citizenship, such as the right to vote or hold office
eligible	qualified, fit to be selected
executive	having to do with the duties and powers of putting laws into effect: *The President is the executive head of the United States Government.*
legislative	having to do with the making of the laws: *Congress is the legislative body for the United States.*
judicial	of, or having to do with, the courts, judges, or the administration of justice
suffrage	the right to vote
revenue	money coming in; income: *Government revenue is supplied by taxes.*
utilities	companies that perform useful public services; bus lines, railroads, and gas and electric companies are utilities
fiscal	financial; having to do with a treasury or exchequer
meteorologist	scientist in the field of weather and the atmosphere
naturalize	admit (a foreigner) to citizenship; make a citizen of an alien
irrigation	supplying the land with water by the use of ditches
reclamation	restoration to a good, useful condition
metropolitan	of or pertaining to a large city: *Metropolitan newspapers are published in Chicago, New York, Los Angeles, and San Francisco.*
economist	person who is a specialist in economics—the science of the production, distribution, and consumption of wealth.

Exercise 50 ◆ CHANGING WORD FORMS

DIRECTIONS ◆ Fill in the blank with the required word or word part.

1. Change *metropolitan* to a noun. Sydney is an Australian

   _____ .   1.___

2. Change *alien* to a verb. The inheritance of a great fortune by one member

   of a family may serve to _____ him from the rest of the
   family.   2.___

3. Exchange the word *consul* for a related word. The official in a foreign city
   who looks out for travelers from his country usually has his office in the

   _____ there.   3.___

4. Change *legislative* to a noun. A member of a legislative body is known as a

   _____ .   4.___

5. Change *maintenance* to a verb. Throughout his college years he was able to

   _____ a high grade point average.   5.___

6. Exchange *eligible* for its antonym. A candidate must meet age, training, and
   experience requirements for a position; otherwise he is declared

   _____ .   6.___

7. Change *reclamation* to a verb. The state _____
   the swamp by draining it.   7.___

8. Change *naturalize* to a noun. Requirements for _____
   include the taking of fingerprints of the applicant.   8.___

9. Change *judicial* to a noun meaning "the system of courts of justice." The branch
   of government that administers justice is known as the

   _____ .   9.___

10. A word related to *disfranchise* and meaning a "right or privilege granted

    by the government" is _____ .   10.___

The key is on page 194.   Your score _____

Exercise 51 ✦ WORDS ENDING IN "OLOGY"

DIRECTIONS ✦ The ending *ology* (from the Greek) means "science or branch of knowledge." Thus *biology* means "the science of living things." On each blank write the word ending in *ology* that is defined at the left. Work to spell the word correctly.

1. science of atmosphere and the weather _____ 1.___

2. study of crimes and criminals _____ 2.___

3. study of the earth's crust, the layers of which it is composed, and their history _____ 3.___

4. study of animals and animal life _____ 4.___

5. the science which seeks to study the mind and discover why people think, act, and feel as they do. _____ 5.___

The key is on page 194. Your score _____

WHIMSICAL WORD ORIGINS[4]

expedite   The Latin *ex* means "out," and *pes, pedis* means "foot." Thus the word means "to free one caught by the foot."

budget   The Romans had a word, *bulga,* meaning "leather bag." The earliest meaning of *budget* was "a pouch or wallet, especially of leather."

Exercise 52 ✦ SUPPLYING THE MISSING WORD

DIRECTIONS ✦ Read each passage and supply the missing word. Use the second blank to correct errors.

1. In making a space capsule or an electronic iron, a submarine or a television set, a bridge or a typewriter, detailed plans are needed to give the exact dimensions and specifications. The workers who draw these plans are

_____ . _____   1.___

2. United States paper money is printed on high-grade paper that is both strong and durable. But even this paper wears out, so the Treasury asks the banks to send in old, worn, torn, or mutilated bills to be exchanged for new ones.

Three-fifths or more of a mutilated bill will be _____ by the Treasurer of the United States for full face value.

_____   2.___

[4] *Picturesque Word Origins* (Springfield, Mass.: G. and C. Merriam Company, 1933), pp. 35, 62.

3. _____ maintain, install, and repair machinery and equipment and examine paper machine rolls, bearings, and pumps to insure that they are in good working condition. They also take apart and reassemble machines and equipment when they are moved about the plant.

_____   3.___

4. It was the purpose of the poll to name the seven greatest construction projects of the Twentieth Century. In a nation filled with spectacular engineering achievements, the task was not easy. What standards should be used for making

judgments? What tests? The engineers' _____ included the usefulness of the project, its value, its beauty, and its size.

_____   4.___

5. From time to time Congress has bestowed United States citizenship upon groups

of people. Through this form of collective _____ ,
citizenship was bestowed upon the inhabitants of Guam, Puerto Rico, and the

Virgin Islands. _____   5.___

6. _____ play an important part in the construction of highways, bridges, dams, and other structures. They provide information on measurements and physical characteristics. They locate land boundaries, assist in setting land valuations, and collect information for maps and

charts. _____   6.___

7. Most cases of bleeding can be controlled by placing a thick, sterile dressing directly over the wound and using firm pressure with the hands. But when

bleeding continues, it may be necessary to apply a _____ .
Wrap a bandage around the limb, tie a half knot, place a stick next to it, and complete the knot. Then twist the stick gently until the bleeding

stops. _____   7.___

8. Crime, filth, crowding, and inconvenience in the big cities are becoming too much for certain companies to endure. In the past four years many large firms have moved their headquarters out of the big cities and others have plans to depart. The figures of the experts indicate that the _____

is speeding up ominously. _____   8.___

9. The problems of severe emotional stress and abnormal behavior, the causes of low morale, or the effective performance of an astronaut in a space capsule

are among the concerns of _____ seeking to understand

people and to explain their actions. Such specialists study the behavior of individuals and groups and often help people to achieve satisfactory personal adjustments. _____ 9.__

10. _____ , the largest group of building trades workers, are employed in almost every type of construction industry. They erect the wood framework in buildings, including subflooring, sheathing, partitions, and rafters. When the building is ready for trimming, they install moulding, wood paneling, cabinets, window sash, doorframes, doors, and hardware, and they build stairs and lay floors. _____ 10.__

11. The newest machines possess human traits that had always in the past been considered far beyond mechanization. Now we find not only electric eyes that see, but many devices that recall and _____ devices that feel. _____ 11.__

12. For countless millions in cities and on farms the telephone is essential. It is an _____ tool of living—in the hour-to-hour conduct of business, in the administration of government, in minor emergencies and great ones, and in maintaining family and community ties.

_____ 12.__

13. Everyone enjoys taking a walk through an attractively designed park or driving along a scenic road. The charm of well-planned campuses, housing projects, country clubs, roads, and parks may stem from the designing of

_____ . _____ 13.__

14. These days sand sailors are often seen scudding across the dry, cracked floor of the desert. Some models weigh only a little more than one hundred pounds and can easily be assembled or disassembled and carried on the rack atop a car. Sand sailor enthusiasts credit much of their popularity to this easy

_____ . _____ 14.__

15. Rainfall, snowfall, sleet, and hail are collectively known as

_____ . This term is derived from a Latin word meaning "to fall headlong." _____ 15.__

The key is on page 195.   Possible score, 30   Your score _____

Give yourself one point for each correct identification and one point for each correct spelling. If you were unable to insert a word, check the key and write the word twice.

Exercise 53 ✦ SPEED OF COMPREHENSION

DIRECTIONS ✦ In each row select the antonym for the key word at the left. Write its letter on the blank. Work rapidly and keep a record of your time.

START ✦

1. ominous	a) sinister	b) pending	c) favorable	d) young	e) fair	1. ___
2. convene	a) prepare	b) review	c) assemble	d) disperse	e) come	2. ___
3. abrupt	a) roused	b) gradual	c) taciturn	d) surprised	e) set	3. ___
4. squander	a) hoard	b) scatter	c) waste	d) lavish	e) give	4. ___
5. eloquent	a) greedy	b) inane	c) spirited	d) chatty	e) catty	5. ___
6. intangible	a) vague	b) sticky	c) substantial	d) filmy	e) gay	6. ___
7. skeptical	a) believing	b) doubting	c) ashamed	d) shy	e) inept	7. ___
8. vindicate	a) absolve	b) clear	c) arrest	d) compare	e) accuse	8. ___
9. courageous	a) strong	b) able	c) fearless	d) cowardly	e) dull	9. ___
10. recede	a) advance	b) restrict	c) resume	d) retire	e) stay	10. ___
11. affront	a) compliment	b) defy	c) insult	d) offend	e) fear	11. ___
12. luxuriant	a) lush	b) profuse	c) sparse	d) rich	e) costly	12. ___
13. lavish	a) confident	b) foolish	c) frugal	d) kindly	e) severe	13. ___
14. affluent	a) wasteful	b) rich	c) careless	d) destitute	e) slow	14. ___
15. foresight	a) prudence	b) vision	c) thought	d) rashness	e) bravery	15. ___
16. principal	a) belief	b) chief	c) little	d) subordinate	e) late	16. ___
17. nimble	a) alert	b) awake	c) active	d) agile	e) awkward	17. ___
18. passive	a) inert	b) sleepy	c) animated	d) deaf	e) bright	18. ___
19. trivial	a) petty	b) useless	c) important	d) slender	e) sad	19. ___
20. adversary	a) colleague	b) enemy	c) opponent	d) agent	e) fiend	20. ___

STOP ✦

The key is on page 195.　　　　　Time _____　　　　　Errors _____

Exercise 54 ◆ SPEED OF COMPREHENSION

DIRECTIONS ◆ In each row select the synonym for the key word at the left. Write its letter on the blank. Work rapidly and keep a record of your time.

START ◆

1. lubricate	a) drive	b) repair	c) grease	d) repaint	e) check	1.___
2. restrict	a) punish	b) confine	c) train	d) quiz	e) charge	2.___
3. asphyxiate	a) cure	b) aid	c) treat	d) suffocate	e) recover	3.___
4. diffident	a) carefree	b) shy	c) talkative	d) dull	e) sickly	4.___
5. novice	a) muffler	b) device	c) expert	d) exhaust	e) beginner	5.___
6. bizarre	a) odd	b) sale	c) threat	d) secret	e) faded	6.___
7. symptom	a) ailment	b) test	c) cure	d) indication	e) fever	7.___
8. hazard	a) trial	b) risk	c) doubt	d) warning	e) pain	8.___
9. demise	a) guess	b) solution	c) service	d) garment	e) death	9.___
10. decrepit	a) noble	b) poor	c) aged	d) ingenious	e) frank	10.___
11. mentor	a) adviser	b) critic	c) companion	d) relative	e) sibling	11.___
12. merit	a) worth	b) rumor	c) gossip	d) talk	e) award	12.___
13. therapeutic	a) curative	b) deadly	c) painful	d) gaseous	e) dying	13.___
14. ominous	a) famous	b) sinister	c) common	d) written	e) adept	14.___
15. eloquent	a) expressive	b) noisy	c) mute	d) wordless	e) timid	15.___
16. abhor	a) adore	b) amuse	c) resist	d) fear	e) abominate	16.___
17. potent	a) weak	b) willing	c) powerful	d) ugly	e) handsome	17.___
18. authentic	a) genuine	b) forged	c) first	d) scrawling	e) legible	18.___
19. dogmatic	a) opinionated	b) clever	c) quiet	d) vicious	e) unsure	19.___
20. vindicate	a) absolve	b) accuse	c) arrest	d) try	e) judge	20.___

STOP ◆

The key is on page 195.   Time _____   Errors _____

Exercise 55 ◆ ANALOGIES

DIRECTIONS ◆ In each series, decide upon the relationship between the first two words. Then write in the parentheses the numbers of the two other words in the series having most nearly the same relationship. Be sure to write the numbers *in the same order of relationship.*

EXAMPLE ◆ elm : tree : : __e__ : __d__

      a) evergreen   b) tall   c) shoe   d) furniture   e) chair

1. flock : sheep : : _____ : _____
   a) bees   b) school   c) herd   d) pack   e) swarm   1. ___

2. compliment : complement : : _____ : _____
   a) seize   b) weight   c) vote   d) wait   e) grasp   2. ___

3. hand : glove : : _____ : _____
   a) shoe   b) coat   c) envelope   d) hat   e) letter   3. ___

4. novice : expert : : _____ : _____
   a) master   b) merchant   c) infant   d) learner   e) applicant   4. ___

5. word : dictionary : : _____ : _____
   a) news   b) reputation   c) surgery   d) library   e) book   5. ___

6. equine : horse : : _____ : _____
   a) feline   b) porcine   c) wolf   d) dog   e) cat   6. ___

7. book : author : : _____ : _____
   a) sailor   b) realtor   c) painting   d) artist   e) inventor   7. ___

8. broker : agent : : _____ : _____
   a) specter   b) ghost   c) adviser   d) salesman   e) actuary   8. ___

9. antidote : poison : : _____ : _____
   a) insomnia   b) infection   c) contagion   d) antiseptic   e) tourniquet   9.___

10. quarterback : athlete : : _____ : _____
   a) fullback   b) pilot   c) doctor   d) wound   e) abrasion   10.___

11. mendacity : lying : : _____ : _____
   a) veracity   b) truth   c) anger   d) fear   e) ignorance   11.___

12. Saturday : Sunday : : _____ : _____
   a) Monday   b) Thanksgiving   c) November   d) today   e) October   12.___

13. tired : exhausted : : _____ : _____
   a) happy   b) sad   c) energetic   d) ecstatic   e) bored   13.___

14. reject : accept : : _____ : _____
   a) steal   b) appraise   c) adversary   d) ally   e) student   14.___

15. fact : opinion : : _____ : _____
   a) news   b) reputation   c) degree   d) habitat   e) character   15.___

16. eloquent : expressive : : _____ : _____
   a) bizarre   b) deft   c) skillful   d) bazaar   e) furtive   16.___

17. quell : incite : : _____ : _____
   a) harangue   b) chatter   c) ignite   d) rant   e) extinguish   17.___

18. soprano : female : : _____ : _____
   a) infant   b) contralto   c) bass   d) tenor   e) male   18.___

19. shortage : surfeit : : _____ : _____
   a) top   b) excess   c) purchase   d) insufficiency   e) total   19.___

20. beginning : ending : : _____ : _____
   a) discussion   b) argument   c) suffix   d) change   e) prefix   20.___

The key is on page 195.   Your score _____

Exercise 56 ◆ SELECTING THE MOST SUITABLE WORD

DIRECTIONS ◆ From the key list, select the best descriptive term and write it on the blank.

boisterous	glib	jocular	mute	petite
demure	gullible	miserly	nonchalant	querulous
eminent	inept	morose	overbearing	versatile

1. At times the manager is domineering, inclined to dictate to the others.

   _____   1.___

2. If a clever, inventive person can do many things well, he is properly described as _____   .   2.___

3. The thoughtful, quiet, serious young woman is _____   .   3.___

4. This man does not appear interested in the matter; he is coolly unconcerned.

   _____   .   4.___

5. One who is easily deceived or cheated is _____   .   5.___

6. When young people are noisily gay and cheerful they are often described as

   _____   .   6.___

7. The person who is sullen, ill-humored, and gloomy is

   _____   .   7.___

8. The person who loves money for its own sake and lives poorly in order to keep what he has is _____   .   8.___

9. The statesman who is distinguished and conspicuous for his services is

   _____   .   9.___

10. People who are silent or unable to speak are often referred to as .

   _____   .   10.___

The key is on page 195.   Your score _____

Exercise 57 ✦ SELECTING THE MOST SUITABLE WORD

DIRECTIONS ✦ Fill in each blank with the most suitable word from the list.

| complimented | contrasted | deteriorated | reimbursed |
| concurred | convened | dissented | subsidized |

1. The student-body officers _____ in the belief that the
award should go to their quarterback.   1.___

2. When the truck was found to be faulty in construction, the manufacturer
_____ the customer for his loss.   2.___

3. As a rule, planes that carry the mail are _____ by the
government.   3.___

4. Unfortunately the product _____; it did not live up to
the good name it had earned when it was first introduced to the public. 4.___

5. Two judges _____ from the opinion of the other three.   5.___

The key is on page 195.   Your score _____

Exercise 58 ✦ GETTING THE MEANING FROM THE CONTEXT

DIRECTIONS ✦ Read each passage and try to determine the meaning of the *italicized* word.
Then fill in the blank. Give the meaning concisely.

1. Often a fixed money charge is made by the government for the use of a highway,
bridge, or waterway. This *toll* is but one of the taxes that pays for the services
of government.

_____   1.___

2. Daniel Webster argued that when the Federal Government acts in accordance
with the powers granted by the Constitution, no state can *nullify* that action.

_____   2.___

3. It is against the law to make or pass fake or false money. One of the duties
of the Secret Service is the investigation and arrest of *counterfeiters*.

_____   3.___

4. Each state constitution indicates how it may be changed. Thus the people in
Nebraska were able to *amend* their state constitution to provide a lawmaking
branch with one legislative body instead of the earlier two legislative bodies.

_____   4.___

5. To convene is to assemble, to call together; to *adjourn* may mean just the opposite.

_____ 5.___

6. Organized action to bring about an election is essential. No matter how good the qualifications of the candidate, his chances for winning are slight without a well-planned *campaign*.

_____ 6.___

7. Some states did not at first approve the Constitution. But when these states were promised that the Constitution would be amended to add certain rights, they took steps immediately to *ratify* the document.

_____ 7.___

8. Congress has the power to lay and collect taxes, duties, imposts, and excises. Perhaps no power of Congress is more important than this *fiscal* power.

_____ 8.___

9. No suspect is under compulsion to convict himself by giving evidence under oath. The Fifth Amendment to the Constitution states that no person in any criminal case shall be forced to *testify* against himself.

_____ 9.___

10. By law the inventor is entitled to certain invaluable protection. Once the government has investigated and approved his application, it reserves for him alone the right to make or sell his invention for a period of years. This *patent* is issued by the Department of Commerce.

_____ 10.___

11. The impost is a tax imposed by the government on certain articles brought into the country for sale or use here. But there is also a tax on the manufacturing, sale, or use of certain articles made, sold, or used within the country. There is an *excise* tax on tobacco, for example.

_____ 11.___

12. Economics deals with the material welfare of mankind and the problems of capital, labor, wages, tariffs, taxes, and so on. The services of the *economist* are therefore indispensible in managing the finances of the country.

_____ 12.___

The key is on page 195.   Your score _____

Exercise 59 ◆ REVIEW

DIRECTIONS ◆ On the blank beside each key word at the right, print the letter of the best definition to be found at the left. Work quickly.

Part A

a) sail, manage, steer a ship

b) admit to citizenship

c) make unfriendly

d) contend, contest

e) clear of suspicion, acquit, absolve

f) restore to a good condition

g) fail to make a payment on time

h) break (a law, rule, etc.)

alienate	1. ___
rehabilitate	2. ___
naturalize	3. ___
compete	4. ___
vindicate	5. ___

Part B

a) system that explodes the fuel inside the cylinders of an engine

b) frame, wheels, machinery of an automobile

c) pedal or lever that causes an increase in speed

d) pipe between cylinders and exhaust

e) hole made by piercing

f) device for mixing air with gas to make an explosive mixture

g) means by which used gasoline or steam can escape from an engine

h) set of car cylinders

exhaust	1. ___
chassis	2. ___
ignition	3. ___
carburetor	4. ___
accelerator	5. ___

Part C

a) having to do with treatment or cure; curative

b) continuing a long time

c) spread by contact with patient or object he touched

d) inventive, gifted, resourceful

e) artless, plain, sincere

f) unfriendly, antagonistic

g) severe, sudden

h) easily read, easily understood

ingenuous	1. ___
ingenious	2. ___
therapeutic	3. ___
contagious	4. ___
chronic	5. ___

a) maker of maps and charts

b) ruler with absolute power

c) cartoonist

d) person trained to plan balanced, nourishing meals

e) person not a citizen of the country in which he lives or visits

f) official foreign representative

g) specialist trained in science of weather and atmosphere

h) underwriter

meteorologist	1.___
consul	2.___
cartographer	3.___
alien	4.___
dietitian	5.___

a) person trusted with the secrets of another

b) rough, coarse fellow

c) accomplice, partner in crime

d) one who buys and sells for others

e) person who figures risks, rates, and premiums for insurance companies

f) driver-salesman

g) one who rents property

h) person receiving insurance or other benefits

beneficiary	1.___
routeman	2.___
confidant	3.___
broker	4.___
actuary	5.___

The key is on page 196.

Your score _____

Section Eight

Exercise 60 ✦ KEY WORDS IN ESSAY
EXAMINATION QUESTIONS

DIRECTIONS ✦ Read each item and decide on the directional word the instructor should include in his question. Write the word on the blank.

compare	discuss	illustrate
contrast	enumerate	justify
criticize	evaluate	summarize
define	explain	trace

1. The general topic is the capitals of the 50 states. What term should the examiner use if he wants them listed? _____   1. ___

2. In a series of talks, an instructor has discussed the occupational outlook for the immediate future. In an examination he wants the students to give the main points in brief form, without details and illustrations. What key term should he use in his question? _____   2. ___

3. What, briefly, has been the history of advertising in the United States during the past fifty years? Which term should appear in the question if the instructor wants the students to describe the progress and the key developments in the order of their occurrence? _____   3. ___

4. Often a word—long in the language—comes into sudden prominence and is used again and again in radio and television talks, in the newspapers, and in everyday conversation. *Ecology* is a word of current importance. But what, precisely, is *ecology?* If the examiner wants a clear, concise meaning, which term should he use in his question? _____   4. ___

5. What are the opportunities for farm workers today? What are the opportunities for people in the building trades? If the differences are to be stressed in the answer, what term should appear in the question?

   _____   5. ___

6. The instructor in a First Aid class wants to make sure the members of the group understand how to apply a tourniquet. If he wishes them to draw and label a chart, what word should be included in the question?

   _____   6. ___

7. End-of-the-year figures point to a sharp decline in employment opportunities in certain occupations. The examiner wants the class to interpret the figures, giving reasons and analyzing causes. What term should give direction to the answer? _____   7. ___

8. In some ways agriculture at the turn of the century was quite different from the agriculture of today. In other ways it was much the same. Any question designed to bring out both similarities and differences should include what

word? _____ 8. ___

9. The topic of taxes has been discussed at length in a business course. The instructor wants the examinees to give good reasons for taxes, and show them to be just and right. What term should he use in his question?

_____ 9. ___

10. "Industries may be viewed in terms of whether they produce goods or whether they produce services." If the questioner wants the students to look at the statement closely, considering it from different points of view, what directive

word should he use? _____ 10. ___

The key is on page 196.   Your score _____

Exercise 61 ◆ WORDS OFTEN CONFUSED

D I R E C T I O N S ◆ On the blank at the right, write the word of your choice.

1. The sun *immerged/emerged* from behind a cloud. _____ 1. ___

2. The weather man's *prophesy/prophecy* was not
   fulfilled.   _____ 2. ___

3. A man of *principal/principle*, he refused to
   agree to the plan of the embezzlers. _____ 3. ___

4. He was *indifferent/diffident*—too shy to
   speak before a group of strangers.   _____ 4. ___

5. His speech did not *effect/affect* me as it did you. _____ 5. ___

The key is on page 196.   Your score _____

List Nine ◆ WORDS FROM BANKING AND BUSINESS

D I R E C T I O N S ◆ Read these words aloud. Make sure you can pronounce them.

WORD	SYLLABLES	PRONUNCIATION
usury	u′ su ry	**YOU′** zhu ree
deficit	def′ i cit	**DEF′** i sit
lien	lien	**LEAN′**
specie	spe′ cie	**SPEE′** shee
testator	tes′ ta tor	**TES′** tay tor

MEANINGS[1]

collateral	stocks, bonds, or other property pledged as securities for a loan; valuable assets that can be deposited as securities for a loan
bond	certificate issued by the government or by a company promising to pay back with interest the money borrowed
teller	bank employee who pays and receives money; one of several employees charged with the handling of money
invoice	an itemized statement of goods bought, showing prices, amounts, and shipping charges
inventory	a listing of merchandise on hand at a given time, with valuations
budget	plan for spending money; estimate of the amount that can be spent, and the amounts to be spent for different purposes in a given time
liability	amount owed; debt; state of being under obligation
proprietor	sole owner
investment	something that is expected to produce a profit or income, or both
contraband	against the law; prohibited; goods imported or exported against the law
usury	lending money at an extremely high or unlawful rate of interest
dividend	share of the profits from a business operation
solvent	able to pay just debts
overdraw	check out more than the amount credited to the individual
promissory	containing an agreement or promise, as in a promissory note
deficit	shortage; amount by which a sum of money falls short
larceny	theft; unlawful taking away and using personal property of another without his permission
lien	legal claim on the property of another for the payment of a debt
testator	one who makes a will
draft	written order to pay
credentials	references; letters of introduction
specie	money in the form of coins; metal money
endorse	write one's name on the back of a check, note, or other document
depositor	one who puts money into the bank
currency	money in actual use in a country

[1] Not all meanings are given.

Exercise 62 ◆ SUPPLYING THE REQUIRED WORDS

DIRECTIONS ◆ Fill in the blank with the required word. Work from memory.

1. What is an antonym for *solvent?* _____ 1.__

2. Change *investment* to a verb meaning to buy something that will produce a profit or income. _____ 2.__

3. Change *overdraw* to a noun: the overdrawing of an account at a bank is referred to as an _____ 3.__

4. A word meaning "sole owner" is _____ 4.__

5. One who makes a will is a _____ 5.__

6. Lending money at an unlawful rate of interest is _____ 6.__

7. If your bank is to cash a check for you, you must first sign your name on the back of it. This is your _____ 7.__

8. If you are unable to pay a debt you owe someone, he may make a legal claim on your property. This claim is called a _____ 8.__

9. The money in use in a country is the _____ 9.__

10. Valuable assets that can be pledged as securities for a loan are known as _____ 10.__

The key is on page 196. Your score _____

Exercise 63 ◆ WRITING ANTONYMS AND SYNONYMS

DIRECTIONS ◆ Write the antonym for each of the following words.

1. convenient _____ 3. savage _____

2. profitable _____ 4. genuine _____

5. precious _____

Write a synonym for each of the following words.

1. veracity _____ 3. violent _____

2. indigent _____ 4. defunct _____

5. chide _____

The key is on page 197.   Possible score, 10   Your score _____

SPELLING DEMONS

Words frequently misspelled by secretarial and office workers are listed below. Check your own spelling competence with them. By now these words are familiar in meaning.

Look at each word and pronounce it. Decide whether there are any hard spots. Note the correct spelling. Then test your competence by covering the word and writing it from memory. Then check. If your spelling is correct and you feel certain of your competence, move on to the next word. If any doubts remain, study the word and write it again. Work rapidly, but work to clear away the difficulties.

privilege	_____	_____	_____
gauge	_____	_____	_____
embarrass	_____	_____	_____
parallel	_____	_____	_____
supersede	_____	_____	_____
changeable	_____	_____	_____
asphyxiate	_____	_____	_____
maintenance	_____	_____	_____

Exercise 64 ◆ COMMON WORD PARTS

DIRECTIONS ◆ Look over the list of familiar word parts and review their meanings (not all meanings are listed). Then explore the everyday words that follow. On the blank at the right print the letter that identifies the meaning.

auto	self	pan	all
con	with, together	re	again, once more, anew, back again
dis	opposite of, reverse of	semi	half
ir	not, opposite of	super	above, over, surpassing

1. By *superhuman* effort, the passenger climbed from the submerged plane and reached the surface of the water.

   a) physical
   b) above what is human
   c) extraordinary
   d) frantic

   1.____

2. The dog was taught to *retrieve* the ball thrown by his master.

   a) guard
   b) carry up hill
   c) find
   d) bring back

   2.____

3. Each department in the factory has its beginners and its *supervisors.*

    a) overseers   c) salesmen

    b) tellers   d) secretaries   3.___

4. The meeting adjourned. There was no further need to *confer.*

    a) bargain   c) talk together

    b) argue   d) economize   4.___

5. He hoped to get the athlete's *autograph.*

    a) attention   c) signature

    b) picture   d) final answer   5.___

6. *Irrelevant* comments by the visitor slowed down the meeting.

    a) nonpertinent   c) too frequent

    b) loud   d) discourteous   6.___

7. From the penthouse window, he could get a *panorama* of the city.

    a) wide, unbroken view   c) splendid impression

    b) good idea   d) slanted picture   7.___

8. He returned home *disillusioned* about theatrical life.

    a) no longer enchanted   c) well informed

    b) wondering   d) enthusiastic   8.___

9. Careful thought caused him to *recant* his statement.

    a) doubt   c) explain

    b) repeat   d) take back   9.___

10. The meaning was clear; there was no need to *recapitulate.*

    a) apologize   c) repeat the main points

    b) back down   d) philosophize   10.___

The key is on page 197.   Your score _____

Exercise 65 ✦ WRITING THE REQUIRED WORD

DIRECTIONS ✦ Read the definition at the left, then fill in the blank. Each answer should begin with one of the word parts in the list (*auto-, con-, dis-, ir-, pan-, re-, semi-, super-*).

1. occurring twice a year   _____   1.___

2. answer, reply   _____   2.___

3. not capable of being turned back   _____   3.___

4. assembly; group of people together   _____   4. __

5. cure-all   _____   5. __

6. occurring twice a week   _____   6. __

7. withdraw, take back (a statement)   _____   7. __

8. the story of one's own life   _____   8. __

9. rudeness; impoliteness   _____   9. __

10. oversee; direct (work or workers)   _____   10. __

The key is on page 197.   Your score _____

A REMINDER

To state that your new car is "great" doesn't tell much about it. Is it spacious or compact? Is it capable of great speed or economical to run? Is it durable or comfortable, or handsome in appearance?

Many good words are used in such a way that they fail to express the meaning that was intended. In working to enrich your vocabulary, have in mind the importance of words that help you to specify.

Exercise 66 ◆ SELECTING THE REQUIRED WORD

DIRECTIONS ◆ The words in the list all express the idea of moving ahead on foot. Read the brief definition at the left of the page, then fill in the blank with the proper word.

hike	stalk
march	stride
patrol	toddle
promenade	trudge
prowl	wander

1. take a long walk or tramp   _____   1. __

2. walk wearily with effort   _____   2. __

3. go about looking for something to eat
   or steal   _____   3. __

4. pursue without being seen or heard   _____   4. __

5. go around to watch or guard   _____   5. __

6. move here and there without any specific
   purpose   _____   6. __

7. walk for pleasure or for show   _____   7. __

8. walk with long steps _____ 8. ___

9. move as soldiers do, in time and with
   steps of the same length _____ 9. ___

10. walk with short, unsteady steps _____ 10. ___

The key is on page 197. Your score _____

Exercise 67 ◆ SELECTING THE REQUIRED WORD

DIRECTIONS ◆ The words in this list name groups of living creatures. Read the brief definition at the left, then fill in the blank.

covey	farrow	litter	shoal
drove	flight	pack	swarm

1. large number, often of fish _____ 1. ___

2. young pigs produced at one birth _____ 2. ___

3. small group of partridges or quail _____ 3. ___

4. group of bees settled in a hive _____ 4. ___

5. number of animals hunting together _____ 5. ___

6. group of birds flying together _____ 6. ___

The key is on page 197. Your score _____

Exercise 68 ◆ SELECTING THE SUITABLE WORD

DIRECTIONS ◆ Think of the meanings of the adjectives in this list. Then read each definition and write in the most suitable word.

beautiful	exquisite	graceful	magnificent
elegant	gorgeous	handsome	pretty

1. pleasing in a feminine way;
   not stately or grand _____ 1. ___

2. beautiful in movement (as a good dancer is) _____ 2. ___

3. stately, splendid, grand _____ 3. ___

4. fine looking (man, for example) _____ 4. ___

5. richly colored, splendid _____ 5. ___

6. lovely, delicate _____ 6. ___

The key is on page 197. Your score _____

Exercise 69 ◆ FINDING ANTONYMS

DIRECTIONS ◆ In each row find the word opposite in meaning to the key word at the left. Write its letter on the blank at the right. Work rapidly.

START ◆

1. adversary	a) opponent	b) acquaintance	c) ally	d) felon	1.___
2. mobile	a) flexible	b) rigid	c) deadly	d) heavy	2.___
3. dubious	a) certain	b) doubtful	c) fearful	d) gloomy	3.___
4. placate	a) delay	b) testify	c) madden	d) appease	4.___
5. novice	a) expert	b) apprentice	c) beginner	d) employee	5.___
6. diligent	a) attentive	b) active	c) alert	d) lazy	6.___
7. taciturn	a) talkative	b) silent	c) stupid	d) unconscious	7.___
8. eminent	a) prominent	b) threatening	c) at hand	d) obscure	8.___
9. overt	a) sly	b) obvious	c) open	d) firm	9.___
10. immigrant	a) alien	b) emigrant	c) consul	d) wanderer	10.___
11. dissent	a) differ	b) quarrel	c) argue	d) agree	11.___
12. diffident	a) confident	b) shy	c) timid	d) alert	12.___
13. decrepit	a) dying	b) weak	c) halting	d) strong	13.___
14. skeptical	a) unsure	b) sarcastic	c) unquestioning	d) doubting	14.___
15. tangible	a) solid	b) common	c) existent	d) intangible	15.___
16. abrupt	a) sudden	b) sharp	c) gradual	d) noisy	16.___
17. ingenuous	a) artless	b) plain	c) crafty	d) sincere	17.___
18. vindicate	a) convict	b) acquit	c) testify	d) warn	18.___
19. exuberant	a) excited	b) abundant	c) sparse	d) extinct	19.___
20. squander	a) spend	b) hoard	c) waste	d) budget	20.___

STOP ◆

The key is on page 197.   Time _____   Your score _____

Exercise 70 ✦ FINDING HOMONYMS

DIRECTIONS ✦ In each row find the homonym for the key word at the left. A homonym is a word having the same pronunciation as another, but a different meaning and, perhaps, a different spelling. Work rapidly.

START ✦

1. principle	a) chief	b) procession	c) principal	d) belief	1.___
2. herd	a) pack	b) school	c) hurdle	d) heard	2.___
3. blue	a) grey	b) scarlet	c) blew	d) bellow	3.___
4. counsel	a) council	b) advice	c) advise	d) charter	4.___
5. weigh	a) consider	b) way	c) weird	d) weight	5.___
6. peace	a) apiece	b) calm	c) silence	d) piece	6.___
7. dear	a) dare	b) drear	c) deer	d) rear	7.___
8. bare	a) bore	b) bear	c) rare	d) rear	8.___
9. assistance	a) help	b) aid	c) assistants	d) succor	9.___
10. stationery	a) fixed	b) mobile	c) station	d) stationary	10.___
11. capital	a) capitol	b) capture	c) cavity	d) caption	11.___
12. residents	a) citizens	b) residence	c) reside	d) precedence	12.___
13. by	a) near	b) inside	c) on	d) buy	13.___
14. new	a) knew	b) modern	c) old	d) never	14.___
15. sight	a) place	b) slight	c) site	d) incite	15.___
16. write	a) type	b) wrong	c) true	d) right	16.___
17. hole	a) whole	b) puncture	c) entire	d) hold	17.___
18. current	a) present	b) currant	c) curry	d) correct	18.___
19. great	a) large	b) small	c) grate	d) fireplace	19.___
20. raze	a) raise	b) build	c) rate	d) race	20.___

STOP ✦

The key is on page 198. Time _____ Your score _____

Exercise 71 ◆ FINDING SYNONYMS

DIRECTIONS ◆ In each row find the word closest in meaning to the key word at the left. Write its letter on the blank at the right. Work rapidly. You should know the meanings of these words instantly.

START ◆

1. insomnia	a) worry	b) energy	c) hunger	d) sleeplessness	1.___
2. overt	a) evident	b) dishonest	c) aged	d) thoughtful	2.___
3. eligible	a) trained	b) qualified	c) athletic	d) continuing	3.___
4. postpone	a) hasten	b) nullify	c) delay	d) replace	4.___
5. pollute	a) defile	b) cleanse	c) consume	d) repaint	5.___
6. broker	a) builder	b) banker	c) agent	d) teller	6.___
7. bizarre	a) queer	b) foreign	c) new	d) salable	7.___
8. convene	a) discuss	b) vote	c) assemble	d) adjourn	8.___
9. proprietor	a) owner	b) seller	c) buyer	d) manager	9.___
10. compute	a) question	b) negate	c) charge	d) calculate	10.___
11. eloquent	a) expressive	b) silent	c) dull	d) tongue-tied	11.___
12. abrupt	a) rude	b) fractured	c) sudden	d) unexpected	12.___
13. dissent	a) decide	b) mail	c) reply	d) disagree	13.___
14. alien	a) enemy	b) foreigner	c) novice	d) fighter	14.___
15. deteriorate	a) break	b) improve	c) worsen	d) fracture	15.___
16. adamant	a) snowy	b) unyielding	c) aged	d) uncertain	16.___
17. contraband	a) stolen	b) poisonous	c) drugged	d) prohibited	17.___
18. deft	a) skillful	b) late	c) odd	d) tricky	18.___
19. archaic	a) frozen	b) solidified	c) ancient	d) perplexing	19.___
20. demise	a) garment	b) dressing	c) guess	d) death	20.___

STOP ◆

The key is on page 198.   Time _____   Your score _____

Exercise 72 ◆ RECALL

DIRECTIONS ◆ Fill in each blank with a word (or a derivative) from one of the lists of business terms. Work from memory.

1. It is not always possible for a financier to decide what he will charge for lending money; if he goes beyond the legal limit he is guilty of

   _____.   1.___

2. At regular intervals a merchant takes _____ , listing the goods on hand item by item, and estimating their worth.   2.___

3. A realtor, wishing to expand his business, may need to borrow money. To guarantee its repayment, he may pledge stocks, bonds or other

   _____.   3.___

4. Anyone who fails to pay on time whatever he owes is guilty of

   _____.   4.___

5. Goods transported illegally over the border of a political unit are

   _____.   5.___

6. The term *specie* refers only to metal money; the term

   _____ is broader; it includes paper money as well.   6.___

7. A garage owner may hold a _____ on the automobile of a customer until that customer pays his bill.   7.___

8. If the government grants a company the right to operate a ferry system between two coastal towns, that right is a _____.   8.___

9. A company that buys and sells for customers, particularly in the real estate field, is in the _____ business.   9.___

10. One who has not the money to pay his debts is _____.   10.___

11. One who pays rent for the privilege of occupying land or property is a

    _____.   11.___

12. If a club with 50 dollars in its treasury spends 100 dollars, it is faced with a _____ of 50 dollars.   12.___

13. One who takes and uses the property of another without permission is guilty

of _____.   13. ___

14. If an insurance company makes a profit and shares that profit with its policy-

holders, it is, in effect, paying _____.   14. ___

15. A written order or demand to pay is known as a _____.   15. ___

The key is on page 198.   Possible score, 15   Your score _____

If your answer at any time differs from the one in the key and you think you are correct, consult your dictionary. Give yourself credit if credit is due.

WHIMSICAL WORD ORIGINS

disaster	This word comes from the Latin *dis* (against) and *astrum* (star). A person with bad luck was often thought to be under the influence of an unfavorable star.
squirrel	This comes from the Greek *skia* (shade) and *oura* (tail). The squirrel is thus "a flash of the tail."
lunatic	An expression that comes to us from the Latin *luna* (moon). Originally the *lunatic* was thought to be "moonstruck."
tulip	A descriptive name that comes from an old Persian word meaning "turban." If you will recall the appearance of a *tulip*, you will appreciate its name.

Section Nine

List Ten • TERMS FROM AVIATION

DIRECTIONS • Read these words aloud. Make sure you can pronounce them.

WORD	SYLLABLES	PRONUNCIATION
fuselage	fu se lage	**FEW'** se lazh or few se **LAZH'**
torque	torque	**TORK'**
hangar	hang' ar	**HANG'** er
parachute	par' a chute	**PAR'** a shoot
altimeter	al tim' e ter	al **TIM'** i ter

MEANINGS[1]

pilot	person who operates the controls and performs other tasks necessary for getting the plane into the air, keeping it on course, and landing it safely. He is called the "captain." He supervises the crew. The copilot is second in command.
altimeter	instrument for measuring the altitude above the earth's surface
flight engineer	one who monitors the operation of the different electrical and mechanical devices on a plane. Before the flight he may check the tires and outside parts of the plane, and make sure the fuel tanks are filled. Once the plane is in the air, he checks instruments and equipment—the air conditioning, for example.
dispatcher	one employed by the airline to coordinate flight schedules and operations within a given area and see that company and safety regulations are observed. He is sometimes called the "flight superintendent."
stewardess	flight attendant on commercial aviation passenger planes; she makes the flight comfortable for the passengers, checks tickets, gives information, makes flight reports, and so on.
mechanic	one who makes emergency repairs on aircraft at a terminal, or takes part in major repairs or periodic inspections at overhaul bases
hangar	structure where airships are housed
propeller	a revolving hub with blades designed to move an airplane
fuselage	the elongated body of the plane
airframe	the plane's fuselage, wings, landing gear, flight controls, and other parts which are not part of the engine, propeller, or instruments
parachute	umbrella-like apparatus for descending safely through the air from a great height
helicopter	wingless aircraft, moving by virtue of its horizontal propellers
aeronautics	science of flying

[1] Not all meanings are given.

astronautics	science of interplanetary flight
torque	force tending to cause rotation
runway	landing strip for planes

GENERAL WORDS

traffic	people, cars, bicycles, ships, or planes moving along a way of travel
duplicate	make an exact copy of; repeat exactly; double
viable	capable of growing and developing; able to keep alive, as *viable plans, viable seeds, viable industries*
humiliate	lower the pride of, lower the self-respect of
nautical	having to do with ships, sailors, and navigation
intolerable	unbearable; too much to be endured
fictitious	imaginary; made up
fallacy	false idea; mistaken belief
versatile	able to do many things well; many-sided; having many abilities

Exercise 73 ✦ COMPLETING ANALOGIES

DIRECTIONS ✦ This is a test of your ability to find the relationship between two words and then call to mind the missing word of a second pair. Fill in the blank with the required word.

EXAMPLE ✦ delay : procrastinate : : restrict : limit

1. speaking : writing : : _____ : libel   1. ___

2. _____ : skill : : pretext : excuse   2. ___

3. recall : foretell : : reminisce : _____   3. ___

4. principal : _____ : : write : right   4. ___

5. wolf : _____ : : bear : ursine   5. ___

6. _____ : therapist : : anesthesia : anesthetist   6. ___

7. _____ : century : : dime : dollar   7. ___

8. plane : _____ : : automobile : garage   8. ___

9. duplicate : _____ : : double : triple   9. ___

10. adaptable : adapt : : tolerable : _____   10. ___

11. _____ : humiliate : : convention : convene   11. ___

12. reject : accept : : _____ : colleague   12. ___

13. vindicate : convict : : disperse : _____   13. ___

14. _____ : talkative : : judicious : rash   14. ___

15. alphabet : letter : : _____ : coin   15. ___

125

16. village : _____ : : brook : river   16.___

17. flour : bakery : : _____ : laundry   17.___

18. monologue : _____ : : one : two   18.___

19. lend : borrow : : _____ : credit   19.___

20. stars : astronomy : : weather : _____   20.___

The key is on page 198.   Your score _____

Exercise 74 ◆ IMPORTANT WORD PARTS

DIRECTIONS ◆ Many English words in common use today are derived from old Latin and Greek words. *Phonograph, telephone,* and *symphony* are all related to the Greek *phon,* which means "sound." *Inspect, introspect,* and *aspect* all include the Latin *spect,* which comes from a Latin verb meaning "to look at." Look closely at the words in each set below, then try to determine the meaning of the word part printed in **boldface** type.

1. motion, motor, motive   mot   _____ 1.___

2. moving, remove, movable   mov   _____ 2.___

3. tenure, tenant   ten   _____ 3.___

4. describe, scribble   scrib   _____ 4.___

5. subscription, postscript   script   _____ 5.___

6. admit, omit, permit   mit   _____ 6.___

7. traction, subtract   tract   _____ 7.___

8. important, porter   port   _____ 8.___

9. verbal, adverb   verb   _____ 9.___

10. emerge, immerge   merge   _____ 10.___

11. inspire, expire   spir   _____ 11.___

12. vision, visible   vis   _____ 12.___

13. revive, vivisection   viv   _____ 13.___

14. advocate, revoke   voc (vok)   _____ 14.___

15. biology, biography   bio   _____ 15.___

16. geology, geography   geo   _____ 16.___

17. manufacture, manual   manu (man)   _____ 17.___

18. sensitive, sensual   sens   _____ 18.___

19. civic, civilian   civ   _____ 19.___

20. annual, annuity   annu   _____ 20.___

The key is on page 198.   Your score _____

Exercise 75 ✦ SPEED OF INTERPRETATION

DIRECTIONS ✦ Place an X in front of each expression which mentions anything that may possess life. Work rapidly. Keep a time record.

EXAMPLE ✦ _____ a new airship

_____X_____ giant watchdog

START ✦

___ 1.	gloom is lifting
___ 2.	save a youngster
___ 3.	in the background
___ 4.	take the course
___ 5.	with no risk
___ 6.	today and tomorrow
___ 7.	for the passenger
___ 8.	pay the worker
___ 9.	no innocent civilian
___10.	shocking accident
___11.	the next day
___12.	fountain pen
___13.	get the point
___14.	severance pay
___15.	not all true
___16.	the best reason
___17.	money for clothes
___18.	for the defendant
___19.	accused of default
___20.	not a chance
___21.	or an auditor
___22.	the weather
___23.	from the tailor
___24.	in the service
___25.	a good secretary
___26.	meteorologist
___27.	cockpit
___28.	only occasionally
___29.	cold and wet
___30.	warm and dry
___31.	not in the autumn
___32.	for the birds
___33.	fleet of ships
___34.	pilot and copilot
___35.	helicopter
___36.	chauffeur
___37.	chassis
___38.	a catch of fish
___39.	the growing shrubs
___40.	swarm of insects

START ✦

___ 1.	with a touchdown
___ 2.	not a football
___ 3.	sports writer
___ 4.	off and on
___ 5.	to the halfback
___ 6.	for the present
___ 7.	tired
___ 8.	without question
___ 9.	another witness
___10.	telephone call
___11.	to a businessman
___12.	clerks and typists
___13.	accountants
___14.	brokers
___15.	proprietors
___16.	only a newcomer
___17.	down and out
___18.	four years ago
___19.	with perfect candor
___20.	offhand
___21.	witty remark
___22.	guardian
___23.	off to work
___24.	no longer an exile
___25.	teachers as well
___26.	soup and dessert
___27.	a Great Dane
___28.	the best answer
___29.	ruined
___30.	infant
___31.	more time
___32.	in a rush
___33.	year's end
___34.	bank balance
___35.	therapist
___36.	routeman
___37.	scout
___38.	coupe
___39.	dispatcher
___40.	one quarter

STOP ✦

Time _____ Errors _____

The key is on page 199.

STOP ✦

Time _____ Errors _____

Exercise 76 ✦ SPEED OF INTERPRETATION

DIRECTIONS ✦ Place an X before each item that mentions something tangible. Could you see it? Could you taste it, feel it, or touch it? Work rapidly.

START ✦

____ 1. now and then
____ 2. in the travel guide
____ 3. happy memory
____ 4. over the river
____ 5. folk remedy
____ 6. intolerable
____ 7. possible
____ 8. a volume on history
____ 9. rapidly developing
____10. cheerleader
____11. suede shoes
____12. diplomacy
____13. forever and a day
____14. course of time
____15. salt water
____16. passing thoughts
____17. in any decade
____18. homemade sweater
____19. peace and tranquillity
____20. thirteenth
____21. nickel and a dime
____22. yesterday
____23. no other opportunity
____24. ration card
____25. from the pushcart
____26. six months
____27. certainly not
____28. an aching foot
____29. sea-level canal
____30. the spokeswoman
____31. both of the ideas
____32. moral issue
____33. prejudiced writings
____34. silly creatures
____35. with a transistor
____36. rights and wrongs
____37. campus unrest
____38. baking soda biscuit
____39. two volunteers
____40. peace and quiet

STOP ✦

START ✦

____ 1. a lighted lamp
____ 2. by telephone
____ 3. in a soft blanket
____ 4. here and there
____ 5. occasionally
____ 6. never
____ 7. pointedly
____ 8. push the button
____ 9. another mystery
____10. long-range result
____11. and the fleet
____12. a broken arm
____13. for the future
____14. sent new supplies
____15. along the coast
____16. senseless
____17. learn to count
____18. hope and fear
____19. a new strategy
____20. with four potatoes
____21. by this time
____22. perhaps not
____23. strong personality
____24. the new commander
____25. on the moon
____26. the fuselage
____27. with kindly feelings
____28. morbid curiosity
____29. wrote the verses
____30. in the schools
____31. tests and examinations
____32. washed his face
____33. the value of iron
____34. department store
____35. buy a newspaper
____36. way of life
____37. fruit and vegetables
____38. like the photograph
____39. instantly
____40. a supermarket

STOP ✦

Time _____ Errors _____
The key is on page 199.

Time _____ Errors _____

Exercise 77 ◆ DETERMINING MEANINGS
THROUGH WORD PARTS

DIRECTIONS ◆ The list below reviews a few word parts. Look over their meanings, then explore the everyday words that follow. On the blank, print the letter that identifies the best meaning.

locu, loqu	to say, speak, or tell
mov, mot	to move
tract	to draw or pull
vers, vert	to turn
viv	to be alive
voc, vok	to call

1. The mayor will *advocate* the passage of the ordinance.

   a) oppose   c) speak in favor of
   b) question   d) announce   1. ___

2. Women have the reputation of being *loquacious.*

   a) quarrelsome   c) talkative
   b) style-conscious   d) timid   2. ___

3. On a farm a *tractor* can do the work of many horses.

   a) helicopter   c) truck
   b) crane   d) engine used for pulling   3. ___

4. The newspaper printed a *vivid* description of the riot.

   a) lively   c) factual
   b) exaggerated   d) horrifying   4. ___

5. In August he *retracted* his offer to buy the business.

   a) repeated   c) made good
   b) withdrew   d) regretted   5. ___

6. The scientists asked for a *colloquy.*

   a) report   c) diagram
   b) conference   d) confirmation   6. ___

7. An insulting remark will *provoke* an angry response.

   a) suggest   c) quash
   b) nullify   d) call forth   7. ___

8. For years he has lived in a *remote* mountain area.

   a) wooded   c) far removed
   b) arid   d) arctic   8. ___

9. Flowers *revive* in water.

   a) look best   c) lose their petals
   b) come back to life   d) droop   9. ___

10. Later the managers *reversed* the budget trend.

    a) looked over   c) implemented
    b) voted on   d) turned back   10. ___

11. He is rarely guilty of *circumlocution*.

    a) lying   c) chattering
    b) boasting   d) roundabout way of talking   11. ___

12. They remained in England for a *protracted* visit with friends.

    a) pleasant   c) long drawn out
    b) unexpected   d) year-long   12. ___

13. The man is a *versatile* genius in the field of art.

    a) absolute   c) many-sided
    b) unknown   d) well advertised   13. ___

14. They may *distract* him from his study.

    a) draw away   c) coax
    b) discourage   d) keep   14. ___

15. These machines *convert* cotton to cloth.

    a) stitch   c) compare
    b) turn   d) glue   15. ___

The key is on page 199.   Number of correct answers _____

Exercise 78 ◆ WRITING SUITABLE
ADJECTIVES AND NOUNS

Part A

DIRECTIONS ◆ Write four adjectives that might properly be used to describe a little girl who is pleasing to watch.

_____   _____   _____   _____

DIRECTIONS ✦ Write four adjectives that might properly be used to describe an unusual costume worn on the street.

_____ _____ _____ _____

Part C

DIRECTIONS ✦ Write four nouns meaning the same or nearly the same as _merchant_.

_____ _____ _____ _____

The key is on page 199.　　　　　Possible score 12　　　　　Your score _____

Exercise 79 ✦ GETTING THE MEANING FROM THE CONTEXT

DIRECTIONS ✦ Read each passage and try to determine the meaning of the _italicized_ word as it is used there. Then fill in the blank. Write the meaning concisely.

1. There had been no rain there for eight months. Young plants died and the shrubs and trees drooped. In the city tanks the water level was low. It was the longest _drought_ in the memory of the old-time dwellers there.

   _____ 1.___

2. It takes little to _humiliate_ some people. Their self-esteem is hurt if they forget for a moment the name of a friend. They are mortified if they fail to keep a minor engagement or misuse a word.

   _____ 2.___

3. He was poor in mathematics, but excelled in dramatics. From the tenth grade on he was the star of all the major plays, with a well-earned reputation for his _histrionic_ skill.

   _____ 3.___

4. Most young girls are interested in friends their own age, in clothes, and in social activities. It seemed _grotesque_, then, that Agatha's room resembled a tool shed.

   _____ 4.___

5. There is not a single "lone wolf" in the group. All of the members are outstandingly _gregarious_.

   _____ 5.___

6. Don rarely had much to say, but his twin was quite different. Dave was the _garrulous_ one, and much of his talk was about trifles.

   _____ 6.___

7. Ex-criminals and lawbreakers often live under assumed names, but many people in good standing also make use of *pseudonyms*.

_____ 7.___

8. He was a businessman, but he did not spend all of his time at work. His chief *avocation* was golf.

_____ 8.___

9. The pirates along the coast would first *pillage* the little homes and then burn them.

_____ 9.___

10. The chairman was firm. He made plain his *implacable* opposition to higher taxes.

_____ 10.___

11. A steady stream of timber, forage, and water from the forests adds strength to the nation's economy. Equally important but less *tangible* public benefits are the recreation opportunities.

_____ 11.___

12. Many companies have moved their headquarters from the city to the suburbs. Some have tried to create a rural atmosphere by planting daffodils, shrubs, and trees on the grounds. One company spent 20 million dollars to preserve the *bucolic* effect.

_____ 12.___

13. In the past the law has generally barred a child from suing his parents for injuries resulting from neglect. But the feeling is now changing. There is a trend to condemn the notion that a parent may act negligently with *impunity*.

_____ 13.___

14. There are three types of *stance*—square, open, and closed. Which one is used depends upon the type of shot being hit. In any one the feet should be comfortably apart so that the player has good balance.

_____ 14.___

15. The general knew the importance of details. He ordered the officers to study the habits of the enemy *meticulously*, and then imitate them.

_____ 15.___

The key is on page 199.   Your score _____

WHIMSICAL WORD ORIGINS

The word *quarantine* is derived from the Latin *quadraginta,* meaning "forty." In order to prevent ships from bringing diseases into a harbor, port authorities formerly required suspect vessels to remain in the harbor 40 days before they were permitted any communication with the shore.

Taxicab comes from the French *cabriolet,* a carriage that bounced like a goat.

Exercise 80 ◆ REVIEW

Part A

DIRECTIONS ◆ Read each brief definition. Then select the word defined and write its number on the blank.

1. Structure where airplanes are housed

   a) warehouse   b) garage   c) auditorium   d) hangar   1.___

2. Wingless aircraft that moves by virtue of horizontal propellers

   a) biplane   b) monoplane   c) helicopter   d) blimp   2.___

3. Umbrella-like apparatus for descending safely from a great height

   a) parachute   b) altimeter   c) aileron   d) cowling   3.___

4. Body of an airplane

   a) chassis   b) caboose   c) hull   d) fuselage   4.___

5. Itemized list of goods or items

   a) installment   b) invoice   c) inventory   d) annuity   5.___

6. Person or company to whom goods are sent

   a) corporation   b) assessor   c) appraiser   d) consignee   6.___

7. To check out more than has been deposited

   a) to overdraw   b) to default   c) to remit   d) to certify   7.___

8. One who makes a will

   a) testator   b) beneficiary   c) trustee   d) litigant   8.___

9. Meeting of political leaders to make plans, choose candidates, and so on

   a) census   b) caucus   c) chorus   d) protectorate   9.___

10. Crime of intentionally setting a fire

    a) foible   b) theft   c) malfeasance   d) arson   10.___

11. The admitting of a foreigner to citizenship

    a) naturalization   b) inoculation   c) vindication   d) disfranchisement   11.___

12. Doctor who treats animals

    a) alienist   b) pediatrician   c) veterinarian   d) dogmatist   12.___

The key is on page 200.   Your score _____

Exercise 81 ◆ REVIEW

Part B

D I R E C T I O N S ◆ Read the brief definition, then select the word that was defined. Write its letter on the blank.

1. Top-ranking representative sent by one government to another

    a) consul   b) counsel   c) ambassador   d) scientist   1.___

2. Person trained in the science of atmosphere and the weather

    a) cartographer   b) cardiologist   c) meteorologist   d) therapist   2.___

3. Person who buys and sells bonds, stocks, or grain, for example, for others

    a) actuary   b) broker   c) teller   d) manufacturer   3.___

4. One whose vocation is that of driver-salesman

    a) routeman   b) client   c) millwright   d) technician   4.___

5. One who fails to meet interest or principal payments on time

    a) litigant   b) defaulter   c) investor   d) solicitor   5.___

6. Person in the insurance business who signs the policy and thus accepts the risk against loss

    a) claims adjuster   b) advocate   c) secretary   d) underwriter   6.___

7. Statistical expert for an insurance company

    a) solicitor   b) teletypist   c) actuary   d) surveyor   7.___

8. One who is a member of a lawmaking body

    a) executive   b) judge   c) legislator   d) constituent   8.___

9. Person employed by an airline to coordinate flight schedules within a given area

   a) dispatcher   b) copilot   c) mechanic   d) flight engineer   9.___

10. One who estimates the value of property for taxes

    a) adjuster   b) accountant   c) actuary   d) assessor   10.___

11. One who is sued in a court

    a) defendant   b) plaintiff   c) executor   d) jury member   11.___

12. Skilled workman: an artist at his trade

    a) apprentice   b) conservationist   c) sentry   d) craftsman   12.___

The key is on page 200.   Your score _____

Section Ten

List Eleven ✦ TERMS FROM THE HEALTH SERVICES

WORD	SYLLABLES	PRONUNCIATION
convalescent	con va les' cent	kon va **LES'** sent
veterinary	vet' er i nar y	**VET'** er i nar ee
laboratory	lab' o ra to ry	**LAB'** ra tor ree
technician	tech ni' cian	tek **NISH'** un
hypodermic	hy po der' mic	high po **DER'** mik
pediatrician	pe di a tri' cian	pe di a **TRISH'** un

MEANINGS[1]

pediatrician	a specialist in the care and diseases of infants and children
convalescent	person recovering from an illness
laboratory	workroom devoted to experimental study in any branch of science
technician	the medical technician performs tests connected with the examination and treatment of the patient; he works under the direction of a specialist in the field
hypodermic	an under-the-skin injection
veterinarian	one skilled in treating diseases and injuries of animals
sanitarium	establishment for the treatment of convalescents or those suffering from lingering diseases
occupational therapist	member of a medical team that selects and directs educational, recreational, and vocational activities to help patients become self-sufficient (the team is guided by the instructions of physicians)
dental hygienist	person who, under the direction of a dentist, cleans teeth by removing stains and calcium deposits, and also polishes teeth
clinic	an institution or station, often connected with a hospital or medical facility, for the examination or treatment of outpatients
intern	doctor acting as resident assistant in a hospital, especially one who has completed a required course of study and is preparing for private practice
orthodontist	dentist who specializes in straightening teeth
hospital administrator	top-level executive in a hospital, responsible for hiring and training personnel, administering the budget, planning for space needs, purchasing supplies and equipment, and providing for laundry and other services
antiseptic	substance that inhibits the action of microorganisms
diagnosis	identification of a disease from a study of the symptoms
cardiac	pertaining to the heart

[1] Not all meanings are given.

practical nurse	one who has passed a licensing examination approved by a state board of nursing. Special training courses are about one year in length. Practical nurses, who assist in the care of patients under the direction of medical personnel, are in great demand, but opportunities for advancement without additional training are limited.
cauterize	burn or sear a wound with a hot iron or caustic substance to prevent bleeding or infection
incision	cut made by a sharp instrument
sanitarian	one who inspects hotels, restaurants, dairies, canneries, swimming pools, and other public places for cleanliness and safety, making tests and, when necessary, recommending corrective action
cerebral	relating to the brain
amputate	cut off (a limb or a portion of a limb)
toxic	poisonous
lesion	injury; hurt
benign	not dangerous; of a mild type or character, as *benign tumors*

Exercise 82 ◆ SUPERFLUOUS WORDS

DIRECTIONS ◆ Some of the items in the exercise include words or expressions that are not needed. Identify these items with an X and cross out the superfluous words.

___ 1. a defunct business no longer operating

___ 2. prehistoric records of great age

___ 3. an informative letter

___ 4. list the assets

___ 5. simultaneous appearances at the same time

___ 6. fatal accidents resulting in death

___ 7. self-made millionaire

___ 8. all the news

___ 9. his autobiography of his life

___10. no unforeseen difficulties

___11. with accurate preciseness

___12. then forecast the event ahead of time

___13. with a hypodermic under the skin

___14. surrounded by water

___15. at year's end

___16. with great caution

___17. little interest in tennis

138

____18. a vacillating policy that wavers

____19. the apex of the triangle

____20. the post-mortem made after death

____21. next Wednesday

____22. that may ensue afterwards

____23. the victorious winner

____24. lunar eclipse of the moon

____25. no adversary

The key is on page 200.   Your score _____

Exercise 83 ◆ NONOBJECTIVE EXPRESSIONS

Some writing is objective, without any bias or slanting. Other writing tends to interpret, possibly to make clear the author's thinking, or perhaps to persuade the reader.

DIRECTIONS ◆ Place an X beside each expression that departs from objectivity by voicing the writer's opinion or judgment.

EXAMPLE ◆ _____ the tenth of May

_____X_____ an inexcusable mistake

START ◆

____ 1. the trade winds
____ 2. the check for ten dollars
____ 3. did not arrive
____ 4. healthy indignation
____ 5. the new road
____ 6. ridiculous vanity
____ 7. to the award winner
____ 8. sham crocodile tears
____ 9. crooked diplomacy
____10. the most beautiful city
____11. obnoxious pride
____12. a broken arm
____13. torn ligaments
____14. a new leader
____15. the superb skill of the artist
____16. with political trickery
____17. with admirable competence
____18. an unfair view of the matter
____19. silly sentimentalism
____20. a self-centered ignoramus
____21. name of college
____22. to answer the question

STOP ◆

START ◆

____ 1. the role of the writer
____ 2. in ten minutes
____ 3. because of stupid prejudice
____ 4. soulful, beautiful eyes
____ 5. deplorable conceit
____ 6. for a cut finger
____ 7. an inspired musician
____ 8. the best of the best
____ 9. with unfortunate greed
____10. died of cancer
____11. with cunning and conniving
____12. a new typewriter
____13. a quarter and a dime
____14. printed in Greek
____15. her all-selfish motives
____16. open-hearted generosity
____17. with unforgivable greed
____18. no other trees
____19. a scientist's answer
____20. a silly round of pleasure
____21. compensation
____22. the organized group

STOP ◆

The key is on page 200.   Errors _____

The key is on page 200.   Errors _____

Exercise 84 ◆ MEANINGS OF WORD PARTS

DIRECTIONS ◆ Fill in the blank with the meaning of the word part.

1. The *pre* in *precocious* means _____ 1. ___

2. The *re* in *reclaim* means _____ 2. ___

3. The *im* in *impolite* means _____ 3. ___

4. The *con* in *conversation* means _____ 4. ___

5. The *contra* in *contradict* means _____ 5. ___

6. The *dis* in *discontent* means _____ 6. ___

7. The *port* in *portfolio* means _____ 7. ___

8. The *mit* in *intermittent* means _____ 8. ___

9. The *inter* in *intermission* means _____ 9. ___

10. The *tran* in *transcribe* means _____ 10. ___

11. The *scribe* in *transcribe* means _____ 11. ___

12. The *temp* in *temporize* means _____ 12. ___

13. The *sub* in *subordinate* means _____ 13. ___

14. The *dict* in *predict* means _____ 14. ___

15. The *pseudo* in *pseudonym* means _____ 15. ___

16. The *re* in *rejuvenate* means _____ 16. ___

17. The *poly* in *polygamy* means _____ 17. ___

18. The *retro* in *retrospect* means _____ 18. ___

19. The *in* in *inept* means _____ 19. ___

20. The *col* in *colleague* means _____ 20. ___

21. The *uni* in *universe* means _____ 21. ___

22. The *ex* in *export* means _____ 22. ___

23. The *omni* in *omnivorous* means _____ 23. ___

24. The *auto* in *automotive* means _____ 24. ___

25. The *ir* in *irreverent* means _____ 25. ___

The key is on page 200.

Number of correct answers _____

Exercise 85 ✦ GETTING THE MEANING
FROM THE CONTEXT

DIRECTIONS ✦ Read the sentences in each group and try to determine the meaning of the italicized word. Then write a concise definition.

1. a) With him, lying was a major *foible.* b) In John's family, the misuse of everyday words is a *foible.* c) Keeping a neat room seemed impossible; untidyness was the boy's *foible.*

   _____ 1.___

2. a) The side trip to Liverpool should have been included in the *itinerary.* b) A good *itinerary* points out in detail the plan of travel. c) Any good travel agent will help you with your *itinerary.*

   _____ 2.___

3. a) The remark was *facetious;* it should not have been taken seriously. b) He was full of *facetious* suggestions; everyone laughed at his stories. c) The judge resented the *facetious* answer to his serious question.

   _____ 3.___

4. a) Here, indeed, was a *misanthrope.* b) He cared nothing for his family, and he had no friends. c) His business associates he mistrusted.

   _____ 4.___

5. a) Much of our information about the universe is gained *vicariously.* b) We know a little about the surface of the moon because of the ventures of the astronauts. c) We know something about the North Pole because of the reports and pictures of those who have traveled there.

   _____ 5.___

6. a) After the death of the wage-earner father, there wasn't enough money for the family. b) For years the children lived on the cheapest of food and wore ragged clothes to school. c) In time they became *inured* to the hardship.

   _____ 6.___

7. a) For 50 miles the river wound its way through mountain country. b) Then it emptied into the sea, becoming part of the inlet. c) It was in this *estuary* that the oil tanker caught fire.

   _____ 7.___

8. a) Active forces are at work in our economy. b) New ways of making things, new things to make, and new patterns of living are causing changes in the

kinds of jobs available. c) Awareness of the *dynamic* changes is essential for both young and old.

_____ 8.___

9. a) There was a time when experience alone carried a lot of weight in an application for a job. b) Experience is still important, but today there is a new requirement—education. c) Much experience can become *obsolete* overnight due to industrial change.

_____ 9.___

10. a) Muscles are meant to be used. b) When they are not used, they deteriorate. c) We are, to a great extent, what our muscles make us—weak or strong, vigorous or *lethargic*.

_____ 10.___

The key is on page 201.   Your score _____

Exercise 86 ◆ SELECTING THE SUITABLE WORD

DIRECTIONS ◆ The words in the list are verbs denoting different kinds of stealing. Fill in the blanks.

blackmail	embezzle	loot	plagiarize	shoplift
burgle	kidnap	pilfer	ransack	swindle

1. take and use as one's own the writing of another   _____ 1.___

2. enter the house of another, usually at night, with the intent to steal   _____ 2.___

3. steal a person by force   _____ 3.___

4. cheat, defraud, get by fraud   _____ 4.___

5. search thoroughly and carry away valuables   _____ 5.___

6. plunder or sack (a conquered city, for example)   _____ 6.___

7. steal goods from a shop while pretending to be a customer   _____ 7.___

8. steal in small quantities   _____ 8.___

The key is on page 201.   Your score _____

Exercise 87 ◆ SELECTING THE SUITABLE WORD

DIRECTIONS ◆ The nouns in this list refer to kinds of writings. Write the most suitable word on the blank at the right.

autobiography   comedy   journal   satire
chronicle   fable   novel   scenario

1. outline of a play or book   _____   1.___

2. tale of fiction of book length   _____   2.___

3. fictitious story with a moral   _____   3.___

4. newspaper or magazine   _____   4.___

5. amusing, light drama   _____   5.___

6. story of a person's life written by himself   _____   6.___

7. record of events in the order in which they occurred   _____   7.___

8. literature used to ridicule   _____   8.___

The key is on page 201.   Your score _____

Exercise 88 ◆ SELECTING THE SUITABLE WORD

DIRECTIONS ◆ The words in this list all refer to farming. Fill in the blanks with the most suitable word.

brooder   furrow   incubator   prairie
fodder   granary   mulch   reaper

1. machine that cuts grain or gathers a crop   _____   1.___

2. storehouse for grain   _____   2.___

3. apparatus for hatching eggs   _____   3.___

4. coarse food for cattle and horses   _____   4.___

5. treeless land covered with grass   _____   5.___

6. straw, grass, or other substance used to protect plant roots   _____   6.___

The key is on page 201.   Your score _____

Exercise 89 ◆ SELECTING ANTONYMS

DIRECTIONS ◆ Select the expression opposite in meaning to that of the italicized word. Print its letter on the blank at the right.

1. a *hazardous* undertaking

   a) foolish
   b) safe
   c) risky
   d) frightening

   1. ___

2. an *abrupt* cessation of the rain

   a) gradual
   b) surprising
   c) sudden
   d) welcome

   2. ___

3. his *eloquent* tale of suffering

   a) expressive
   b) emotional
   c) meaningless
   d) resentful

   3. ___

4. with no *tangible* evidence

   a) worthy
   b) material
   c) intangible
   d) credible

   4. ___

5. a *diffident* secretary

   a) confident
   b) efficient
   c) trustworthy
   d) loud-talking

   5. ___

6. *taciturn* as a frightened child

   a) timid
   b) talkative
   c) active
   d) resentful

   6. ___

7. *covert* glances from one to the other

   a) secret
   b) angry
   c) overt
   d) occasional

   7. ___

8. getting used to *urban* life

   a) rural
   b) prison
   c) outdoor
   d) married

   8. ___

9. *eligible* to take the examination

   a) prepared
   b) unwilling
   c) enrolled
   d) ineligible

   9. ___

10. a *skeptical* expression

    a) unfriendly
    b) unquestioning
    c) disinterested
    d) contemptuous

    10. ___

The key is on page 201.   Number of correct answers _____

Exercise 90 ◆ SELECTING SYNONYMS

DIRECTIONS ◆ Select the expression nearest in meaning to that of the italicized word. Print its letter on the blank at the right.

1. with *ominous* implications

   a) merry
   b) optimistic
   c) threatening
   d) puzzling

   1.____

2. *overt* approval of the plan

   a) grudging
   b) uncertain
   c) evident
   d) partial

   2.____

3. the *currency* of the realm

   a) money in use
   b) laws
   c) customs
   d) boundaries

   3.____

4. a *formidable* monster

   a) possessing claws
   b) strange, unfamiliar
   c) fearful
   d) prehistoric

   4.____

5. wanting in *stability*

   a) firmness
   b) training
   c) character
   d) courage

   5.____

6. the *deterioration* of his health

   a) analysis
   b) worsening
   c) discussion
   d) importance

   6.____

7. a reputation for *mendacity*

   a) laziness
   b) hard work
   c) lying
   d) greediness

   7.____

8. including a *warranty*

   a) guarantee
   b) book of rules
   c) discount
   d) gratuity

   8.____

9. reported the *casualty*

   a) fatal accident
   b) unfortunate accident
   c) automobile wreck
   d) arrest

   9.____

10. a *viable* plan

   a) two-way
   b) capable of developing
   c) diversified
   d) impractical

   10.____

The key is on page 201.

Number of correct answers _____

Exercise 91 ◆ REVIEW

DIRECTIONS ◆ Which is the best answer? Indicate your choice by writing the letter on the blank at the right.

1. The word *toxic* means

   a) spread by contact   b) poisonous   c) actual, real   1.___

2. A term meaning "burn or sear a wound to prevent bleeding or infection" is

   a) anesthetize   b) amputate   c) cauterize   2.___

3. As a rule, the purchasing of hospital supplies and equipment is the responsibility of the

   a) resident intern   b) administrator   c) head nurse   3.___

4. Unusual sensitivity to a particular substance, such as cat fur, is known as

   a) an allergy   b) a concussion   c) a lesion   4.___

5. In the words *aquarium, sanitarium,* and *solarium,* the ending *arium* means

   a) clinic   b) surgery   c) place for   5.___

6. The term *cardiac* refers to the

   a) heart   b) lungs   c) brain   6.___

7. The ending *ist* in the words *orthodontist, therapist,* and *hygienist* means

   a) one who practices   b) relating to   c) assistant to   7.___

8. In an essay examination question, the word *enumerate* means

   a) talk over, discuss   b) make clear   c) list   8.___

9. An antonym for *humiliate* is

   a) shame   b) defy   c) dignify   9.___

10. A word meaning "capable of keeping alive, capable of developing" is

    a) benign   b) viable   c) officious   10.___

11. One who pays rent for occupying the property of another is a

    a) proprietor   b) cartographer   c) tenant   11.___

12. The person who, under the supervision of a dentist, cleans teeth is

    a) an orthodontist   b) a practical nurse   c) a dental hygienist   12.___

13. An under-the-skin injection is a

    a) tourniquet   b) hypodermic   c) poultice   13.___

14. A word meaning "curative" or "having curative value" is

    a) chronic   b) acute   c) therapeutic   14.___

15. Something that causes loss of feeling for pain, touch, and cold is

    a) an antiseptic   b) an antidote   c) an anesthetic   15.___

16. In the word *hypodermic,* the meaning of *hypo* is

    a) long-time   b) under   c) skin   16.___

17. A word meaning "inability to sleep" is

    a) insomnia   b) malnutrition   c) anemia   17.___

18. A word meaning "pertaining to the brain" is

    a) dermal   b) cerebral   c) abdominal   18.___

19. A decision based on symptoms about the nature of a disease is a

    a) remedy   b) diagnosis   c) prescription   19.___

20. The ending *itis—appendicitis, tonsillitis—*means

    a) inflammation of   b) full of   c) abounding in   20.___

The key is on page 201.   Your score _____

Exercise 92 ◆ SUFFIXES AND PREFIXES

1. The *ify* at the end of *fortify, magnify,* and *justify* means

   a) make, cause to be   b) build   c) supply   1.___

2. The *ab* in *abnormal, abstract,* and *abduct* means

   a) away, from   b) to, toward   c) drawn   2.___

3. The *ad* in *advance, advocate,* and *adhere* means

   a) in, with   b) to, toward   c) back, again   3.___

4. The *al* in *constitutional, rental,* and *critical* means

   a) act of   b) place for   c) relating to   4.___

5. The *or* at the end of *inventor, debtor,* and *generator* means

    a) native to   b) one who, that which   c) following   5. ___

6. The *multi* in *multimillionaire* and *multilateral* means

    a) wealthy   b) two, double   c) many   6. ___

7. The *un* in *unconscious* means

    a) sleeping   b) waking   c) not   7. ___

8. The *bene* in *benefit* and *benevolent* means

    a) good, well, kindly   b) ill, dangerous   c) again   8. ___

The key is on page 202.   Your score _____

Exercise 93 ◆ SPELLING REVIEW

DIRECTIONS ◆ On the blank at the left, write the word that is defined. Give careful attention to your spelling. For the time being, leave the second blank unmarked.

1. Person who receives money or property from a will or insurance policy

    _____   _____ 1. ___

2. Maker of maps or charts

    _____   _____ 2. ___

3. Person trained in the science of atmosphere and the weather

    _____   _____ 3. ___

4. Physician who specializes in the care of infants and children

    _____   _____ 4. ___

5. Patient recovering from an illness

    _____   _____ 5. ___

6. Expert who figures rates, risks, and premiums for insurance companies

    _____   _____ 6. ___

7. Person who, under the supervision of a dentist, cleans teeth

    _____   _____ 7. ___

8. Top-ranking representative of one government to another

_____   _____   8. __

9. Doctor or surgeon who treats animals

_____   _____   9. __

10. Expert in planning and preparing appetizing and nutritious meals

_____   _____   10. __

The key is on page 202. If you have misspelled any word, write the correct spelling on the second blank. Then work rapidly but effectively to master the correct spelling. Score yourself on your first spelling.

Your score _____

WORDS OFTEN MISSPELLED

Everday words that are often misspelled are included in the following list. Give corrective attention to any that are troublesome to you.

occurrence	separate	gauge
noticeable	liquefy	supersede
advantageous	desirable	parallel
embarrassing	accommodate	privilege

Section Eleven

List Twelve

Part A ◆ GENERAL WORDS[1]

gregarious	fond of being with others, as, for example, *gregarious* kindergartners
paradox	apparent contradiction; statement that seems to say two things opposite in meaning, such as "more haste, less speed"
bucolic	pastoral, rural, rustic, such as a *bucolic* setting for a play
monologue	long speech by one person in a group; part in a play in which a single actor speaks alone
precarious	risky, not safe, as a *precarious* position on the ice
contemptuous	scornful, showing the feeling that a person, act, or thing is low, mean, or worthless
diminutive	tiny, small
incredulous	showing lack of belief; unwilling to believe
overbearing	domineering; forcing others to do one's will
pessimistic	tending to take a gloomy view or looking at the dark side of life

Part B ◆ WORDS FROM THE BUILDING TRADES

architect	person who designs buildings and sees that the plans are carried out
contractor	one who undertakes to do certain work, such as putting up a building. General contractors take full responsibility for the whole job (like building a bridge); special-trade contractors do the work of only one trade, perhaps painting, carpentry, plumbing, or heating.
journeyman	workman who knows his trade
foreman	man in charge of a group of workers
mortar	mixture of lime, sand, and water for holding bricks or stones together
glazier	person whose work is putting glass in window frames, picture frames, and generally working with glass
blueprint	photograph that shows white outlines on a blue background, commonly used to make copies of the architect's plans
buttress	support built against a wall or building to strengthen it
clapboard	narrow boarding on the outside of a house
scaffold	temporary structure or framework for holding workmen or materials
apprentice	one who is learning an art, trade, or calling under skilled workers

Part C ◆ WORDS FROM RADIO AND TELEVISION

affiliated (stations)	associated; connected
network	group of stations working together
station manager	one who may act as business and sales manager, script writer, program director, and even announcer

[1] Not all meanings are given.

programming department	department that plans, prepares, and produces radio and television shows
announcer	one who introduces programs, guests, and musical selections, and often delivers live commercial messages
newswriter	one who selects and writes news copy to be read on the air
newscaster	one who broadcasts the daily news programs and reports special news events on the scene
audition	trial record or hearing
script	manuscript used for a broadcast
sponsor	one who pays for a program

Part D ◆ WORDS FROM CLERICAL AND RELATED OCCUPATIONS[2]

stenographer	The stenographer takes dictation and transcribes her notes on a typewriter. Most stenographers record their notes in shorthand.
secretary	In addition to stenographic work, the secretary relieves the employer of numerous routine duties and often handles business details on her own initiative.
typist	The typist operates the typewriter, the machine found in almost any office, producing typed copies of written and printed materials.
receptionist	The receptionist receives and gives information to customers and other people who telephone or call. It is her job to find the nature of the caller's business and then direct him to the proper official.
bookkeeper	The bookkeeper records day-by-day business transactions in journals, ledgers, and other accounting forms. At intervals he prepares summary statements showing, for example, money taken in and paid out by the firm, from whom it came, and to whom it went.
cashier	Nearly all cashiers receive payments made by customers for goods and services. Records of the amount of money involved in each transaction are kept so that cash accounts can be balanced at the end of the day. (Duties vary from job to job, and so do titles—for example, checkout clerk, credit cashier, bill-clerk, cashier-checker.)
office machine operator	The types of machines used to speed up the paper work in modern business are highly varied. Many of the operators have titles taken from the kinds of equipment they use. A few examples are the key punch operator, the billing machine operator, and the calculating machine operator.
shipping clerk	The shipping clerk does the clerical work that enables business firms to keep track of goods shipped from one place to another.
sales clerk	The sales clerk waits on customers, wraps articles, prepares sales slips, and makes change.
salesperson	The salesperson displays, explains, and sells merchandise in addition to performing the tasks described for the sales clerk.

[2] *Occupational Outlook Handbook, Career Information for Use in Guidance,* Bulletin No. 1450, U. S. Department of Labor (Washington, D. C.: U. S. Government Printing Office, 1967), pp. 278–302.

Exercise 94 ◆ SPEED OF INTERPRETATION

DIRECTIONS ◆ Place an X before each expression which mentions anything that may possess life. Work rapidly.

START ◆

___ 1. fed the pony
___ 2. another day
___ 3. in the stable
___ 4. says the writer
___ 5. the strength of a horse
___ 6. still adrift
___ 7. one observer
___ 8. in the stone age
___ 9. another critic
___10. having the effect
___11. passenger planes
___12. the gasoline problem
___13. with the bill
___14. employ a peasant
___15. not a prince
___16. add and subtract
___17. always a patriot
___18. made of steel
___19. initial success
___20. found the orphan
___21. only a myth
___22. mud and slime
___23. in a notebook
___24. yield
___25. ounce of prevention
___26. and the operator
___27. in a panic
___28. a patient now
___29. and a surgeon
___30. pageant or parade
___31. comic version
___32. father of the king
___33. once a musician
___34. no opportunity
___35. a maker of films
___36. on business
___37. next month
___38. October
___39. to the reader
___40. a computer

STOP ◆

START ◆

___ 1. better equipment
___ 2. a mechanic
___ 3. for a wolf hound
___ 4. no mosquitoes
___ 5. with baked potatoes
___ 6. for the prisoner
___ 7. hot summer days
___ 8. autumn leaves
___ 9. principal
___10. a true supporter
___11. pay the price
___12. on the campus
___13. historic in nature
___14. but no passengers
___15. a new idea
___16. to find a porcupine
___17. the principle
___18. health checkup
___19. career diplomat
___20. dietitian
___21. to the pygmy
___22. a stream with reptiles
___23. the incumbent
___24. always a glutton
___25. no credit
___26. without money
___27. and no excuse
___28. possibly tomorrow
___29. an itinerant
___30. fumigate the house
___31. flippant attitude
___32. possibly an imposter
___33. expose the trick
___34. the jargon of thieves
___35. to be an informer
___36. a brush and comb
___37. he and his wife
___38. round the clock
___39. to the laundry
___40. now and then

STOP ◆

Time _____ Errors _____

The key is on page 202.

Exercise 95 ✦ SPEED OF INTERPRETATION

DIRECTIONS ✦ Place an X before each expression that includes a noun.

START ✦

___ 1. 52 weeks
___ 2. letters
___ 3. to report
___ 4. squinting sleepily
___ 5. wanting to improve
___ 6. renew the fight
___ 7. bowing low
___ 8. can be called
___ 9. have an influence
___10. fears grew
___11. unilaterally
___12. now and then
___13. slowly
___14. somewhat later
___15. nor deny
___16. he will answer
___17. they believe
___18. suit their tastes
___19. well protected
___20. new pollutants
___21. statisticians
___22. left to die
___23. with no desire
___24. barter is permitted
___25. profit
___26. not content
___27. currently
___28. now possible
___29. your picture
___30. is always adding
___31. some people
___32. fully aware
___33. kept wading in
___34. know your roadways
___35. the guessing game
___36. once more
___37. a master machinist
___38. sweeping floors
___39. to leave soon
___40. his hobby

STOP ✦

START ✦

___ 1. in the preface
___ 2. look out the window
___ 3. yours truly
___ 4. cordially
___ 5. in retrospect
___ 6. the tail wags
___ 7. above a certain age
___ 8. a new campus
___ 9. unfinished
___10. inside and out
___11. negative benefits
___12. and say further
___13. authentic
___14. with lumpy arms
___15. still living
___16. breathing slowly
___17. a new idiom
___18. finished quickly
___19. with skill
___20. an old penny
___21. in the negative
___22. stupidly
___23. not too early
___24. then collapses
___25. not immediately
___26. searching and finding
___27. younger than springtime
___28. eminently logical
___29. closed in the fall
___30. red and blue
___31. came ambling out
___32. shifted
___33. the first jets
___34. moved away
___35. very cagily
___36. to the tower
___37. came to a halt
___38. drawn out
___39. the plot thickens
___40. fourth and fifth days

STOP ✦

Time _____   Errors _____

Time _____   Errors _____

The key is on page 202.

Exercise 96 ✦ GETTING THE MEANING
FROM THE CONTEXT

DIRECTIONS ✦ Read each passage and try to get the meaning of the *italicized* word. Then fill in the blank. Give the meaning concisely.

1. Occasionally a selfish person does little or no work yet receives a good salary. But most professional people would scorn such a *sinecure*.

   _____ 1. ___

2. Good neighborliness between two countries does not always reflect a selfish concern for good business. Today the chances are good that it reflects as well an *altruistic* concern of one country for the welfare of another.

   _____ 2. ___

3. Where his efforts will take him is a matter of *conjecture*. There is talk that he would like to be the governor of his state or a member of the United States Senate. At the moment he is working on a thesis in the field of political science.

   _____ 3. ___

4. Discipline is essential in military life. Many commanders of ships and bases believe that no one has the right to delve into matters that have long been their rightful *prerogatives*.

   _____ 4. ___

5. I now had a clear view of the whole college field and of the tall weeping willows. Lying expressionless and contented were six black cows, whose appearance on the college grounds reminded me that even so *erudite* an institution as this might have a rural setting.

   _____ 5. ___

6. He never learned to spell. But though he was no great shakes on *orthography* he possessed a fine sense of drama, and the record of his trip is the best travel story I have ever read.

   _____ 6. ___

7. As a rule, the indentured servant was a man *inured* to hard physical labor who expected to work all his life, and had little interest in the graces and amenities of the wealthy.

   _____ 7. ___

8. Indeed, it is not unheard of for a candidate to interpret his platform in opposite ways, depending on whether he is speaking in New York or in Idaho. No

language has yet been devised that a *devious* man cannot use in devious ways, but the English language lends itself to that sort of thing exceptionally well.

_____ 8. ___

9. The beach had a *jetty* of its own—firm, safe, and solid. It was built well out into the water and served as an excellent pier for our dinghy.

_____ 9. ___

10. The historian, while relishing the excitement of the adventure, remains unsatisfied until he *penetrates* into the broad factor of causation.

_____ 10. ___

The key is on page 202.   Number of correct answers _____

Exercise 97 ✦ FINDING SYNONYMS

DIRECTIONS ✦ Look at the key word at the left. Then, from the group of words at the right, select the one that is closest in meaning. Write its letter on the blank.

1. squander	a) save	b) distribute	c) hoard	d) waste	1. ___
2. ingenuous	a) clever	b) artful	c) sincere	d) crafty	2. ___
3. alien	a) traveler	b) foreigner	c) officer	d) victim	3. ___
4. pedestrian	a) driver	b) walker	c) adviser	d) acquaintance	4. ___
5. demise	a) guess	b) journey	c) death	d) property	5. ___
6. convene	a) assemble	b) discuss	c) elect	d) admire	6. ___
7. restrict	a) advise	b) confine	c) patrol	d) promise	7. ___
8. lubricate	a) grease	b) make up	c) fabricate	d) abscond	8. ___
9. loathe	a) fear	b) detest	c) love	d) admire	9. ___
10. antidote	a) operation	b) remedy	c) poison	d) capsule	10. ___
11. eloquent	a) inane	b) meaningless	c) diffident	d) expressive	11. ___
12. therapeutic	a) painless	b) diagnostic	c) curative	d) manipulative	12. ___
13. abhor	a) abominate	b) like	c) envy	d) admire	13. ___
14. casualty	a) accident	b) threat	c) menace	d) happening	14. ___
15. voracious	a) greedy	b) generous	c) feline	d) fierce	15. ___
16. metropolitan	a) elegant	b) wealthy	c) crowded	d) urban	16. ___
17. raze	a) build	b) construct	c) lift	d) destroy	17. ___
18. proprietor	a) druggist	b) grocer	c) owner	d) watchman	18. ___

19. skeptical	a) amused	b) doubtful	c) sarcastic	d) aroused	19.___
20. audacity	a) stability	b) annuity	c) veracity	d) boldness	20.___
21. wily	a) dishonest	b) skillful	c) precocious	d) crafty	21.___
22. employ	a) train	b) hire	c) read	d) serve	22.___

The key is on page 203.   Possible score, 22   Your score _____

Exercise 98 ✦ FINDING ANTONYMS

DIRECTIONS ✦ Look at the key word at the left. Then, from the group of words at the right, select the one that is opposite in meaning. Write its letter on the blank.

1. incredulous	a) believable	b) credible	c) ignorant	d) credulous	1.___
2. deft	a) hearing	b) artful	c) clumsy	d) clever	2.___
3. terminate	a) irrigate	b) end	c) begin	d) enclose	3.___
4. diligent	a) lazy	b) interested	c) tired	d) arrogant	4.___
5. tangible	a) heavy	b) wooden	c) silent	d) intangible	5.___
6. pessimistic	a) sad	b) optimistic	c) ready	d) angry	6.___
7. occupy	a) evacuate	b) buy	c) well	d) furnish	7.___
8. contemptuous	a) scornful	b) admiring	c) proud	d) haughty	8.___
9. precarious	a) secure	b) risky	c) bizarre	d) slow	9.___
10. diminutive	a) little	b) tiny	c) childish	d) great	10.___
11. enlarge	a) condense	b) add	c) refill	d) grow	11.___
12. spread	a) contract	b) open	c) retell	d) gossip	12.___
13. exhaust	a) spend	b) drain	c) tire	d) replenish	13.___
14. ominous	a) favorable	b) sinister	c) coming	d) untidy	14.___
15. minority	a) majority	b) many	c) some	d) all	15.___
16. rigid	a) stiff	b) fixed	c) firm	d) flexible	16.___
17. poverty	a) want	b) need	c) wealth	d) hunger	17.___
18. purchase	a) sell	b) rent	c) buy	d) acquire	18.___
19. barren	a) dry	b) rocky	c) fertile	d) grassy	19.___
20. arrive	a) come	b) visit	c) travel	d) depart	20.___
21. praise	a) admire	b) approve	c) blame	d) copy	21.___
22. immense	a) minute	b) large	c) great	d) huge	22.___

The key is on page 203.   Possible score, 22   Your score _____

DIRECTIONS ◆ Words similar in sound are often confounded. Look closely at the following pairs of words and contrast their meanings. Then complete each sentence by writing in the correct word from this list.

affect	coarse	disease
effect	course	decease
bullion	counsel	miner
bouillon	council	minor

1. The city _____ met to discuss the new zoning laws.   1.___

2. The meals at the dormitory always include soup; the favorite is

   _____ .   2.___

3. The early _____ of the father left the children with insufficient funds for their education.   3.___

4. It was the hope of both students and faculty that the content of the

   _____ would be changed.   4.___

5. The explosion took place at night well below the surface of the earth; fortunately there was not a single coal _____ on duty at the time.   5.___

6. Uncoined silver and gold, usually in ingots, are known as

   _____ .   6.___

7. A doctor gives his patients good _____ .   7.___

8. Penalizing any player is bound to _____ the rest of the team.   8.___

9. The scientists were encouraged by their findings; a cure for the

   _____ at last seemed possible.   9.___

10. A person under the legal age of responsibility is a _____ .   10.___

11. A widely advertised "remedy," it had little or no _____ on some patients.   11.___

12. Unfortunately good ideas are often disguised by _____ , unrefined language.   12.___

13. A cut on the hand may be a _____ injury, unless an infection develops.   13.___

14. Lack of sleep may _____ the ability to think clearly.   14.___

15. Demise and _____ are synonyms.   15.___

The key is on page 203.   Your score _____

Exercise 100 ◆ CHOOSING THE CORRECT WORD

DIRECTIONS ◆ Fill in each blank with the word defined briefly at the left.

bake	boil	fry	simmer
barbecue	broil	parboil	toast

1. cook in a pan or on a griddle in hot fat   _____   1.___

2. boil until partly cooked   _____   2.___

3. cook by putting or holding near a fire   _____   3.___

4. cook by dry heat, as in an oven, without exposing directly to the fire   _____   4.___

5. roast or broil whole, or cook before an open fire   _____   5.___

6. cook a fluid or in a fluid with the liquid bubbling up and giving off steam   _____   6.___

7. keep at or just below the boiling point   _____   7.___

8. brown by heat   _____   8.___

The key is on page 203.   Your score _____

Exercise 101 ◆ SUPPLYING THE CORRECT WORD

DIRECTIONS ◆ On the blank, write the verb defined at the left. Each verb has to do with the use of money.

1. give (money) or leave it by will   _____   1.___

2. use (money) to buy something that is supposed to produce profit or an income, or both   _____   2.___

3. receive or deserve (money) for work or service   _____   3.___

4. let another have or use (money) for a time   _____   4.___

5. give (money) along with others; furnish as a share _____ 5.___

6. spend foolishly; waste _____ 6.___

7. promise to give or pay (a sum of money) _____ 7.___

8. get from another person with the understanding that it must be returned _____ 8.___

The key is on page 203.   Number of correct answers _____

Exercise 102 ◆ SUPPLYING THE CORRECT WORD

D I R E C T I O N S ◆ On the blank write the adjective defined at the left. Each adjective is descriptive of a human trait.

1. mentally advanced; developed earlier than usual _____ 1.___

2. timid, shy, bashful _____ 2.___

3. astute; clever in practical or business affairs _____ 3.___

4. gifted, having natural ability _____ 4.___

5. able to do many things well _____ 5.___

6. having good knowledge and good judgment _____ 6.___

7. scholarly, having much knowledge _____ 7.___

8. hard working, industrious _____ 8.___

The key is on page 203.   Number of correct answers _____

Exercise 103 ◆ SUPPLYING THE REQUIRED WORD

D I R E C T I O N S ◆ Listed below are a few Latin and Greek word parts. Not all of them are new to you. Look over the list, then go on to fill in the blanks. Use words that are made up from one or more of these word parts.

credere	believe, trust
grex, gregis	flock, herd, company
mono, mon	of, by, or with but one; one, single, alone
post	behind, back, or after in position
sent, sens	feel
spectare, spectus	look at
tele	distant
vid, vis	see

1. instrument for producing sounds, especially speech, at a distance or from a distant point

_____ 1.___

2. fond of being with other people

_____ 2.___

3. disagree, feel a difference of opinion

_____ 3.___

4. without change or variety; varying little in tone; wearisomely uniform

_____ 4.___

5. not willing to believe

_____ 5.___

6. management, oversight, direction

_____ 6.___

7. group of people, or flock of people gathered together

_____ 7.___

8. occurring after death

_____ 8.___

9. examine one's own thoughts

_____ 9.___

10. feeling (for cold, pain, heat)

_____ 10.___

The key is on page 203.

Number of correct answers _____

Exercise 104 ◆ REVIEW

DIRECTIONS ◆ Which word is defined? Indicate your choice by writing the letter on the blank at the right.

1. A person whose work is putting glass in window frames and picture frames is a (an)

   a) auditor b) sentry c) glazier d) assessor 1.___

2. The device by which used gasoline or steam escapes from an engine is the

   a) carburetor b) muffler c) accelerator d) exhaust 2.___

3. A wolflike creature is

   a) lupine b) vulpine c) porcine d) equine 3.___

4. A descriptive term for a person enfeebled by the infirmities of age is

   a) antique b) decrepit c) archaic d) obsolete 4.___

5. A word meaning "lasting a long time" is

   a) acute b) fatal c) infectious d) chronic 5.___

6. A creature that eats only plant food is

    a) herbivorous   b) omnivorous   c) carnivorous   d) voracious   6.___

7. The person who takes dictation and transcribes the notes is a

    a) receptionist   b) cashier   c) typist   d) stenographer   7.___

8. The body of an airplane is the

    a) fuselage   b) chassis   c) propeller   d) altimeter   8.___

9. An injury to the brain or spine caused by a sudden blow, shock, or fall is a (an)

    a) concussion   b) transfusion   c) infection   d) contagion   9.___

10. Stocks, bonds, and other properties pledged as security for a loan constitute

    a) collateral   b) dividends   c) premiums   d) policies   10.___

11. A device to stop bleeding by compressing a blood vessel is a (an)

    a) poultice   b) tourniquet   c) symptom   d) anesthetic   11.___

12. A person who designs buildings and sees that the designs are carried out is a (an)

    a) contractor   b) architect   c) promoter   d) adjuster   12.___

13. A fundamental belief or rule for action is a (an)

    a) announcement   b) principal   c) axiom   d) principle   13.___

14. One who pretends to be ill to get out of a duty is guilty of

    a) slander   b) larceny   c) malingering   d) libel   14.___

15. If an examiner wants his students to stress unlikenesses or dissimilarities of things, events, or qualities, his question should be built around the word

    a) trace   b) compare   c) evaluate   d) contrast   15.___

16. A statement that seems to say two things opposite in meaning is a

    a) monologue   b) satire   c) chronicle   d) paradox   16.___

17. A word meaning "being fond of others" or "liking to be with others" is

    a) tractable   b) skeptical   c) dubious   d) gregarious   17.___

18. The person who does the clerical work that enables business firms to keep track of goods shipped is a

    a) sponsor   b) shipping clerk   c) secretary   d) auditor   18.___

19. A temporary structure for holding workmen or materials for a building operation is a

    a) buttress   b) casement   c) portico   d) scaffold   19.___

20. A photograph of the architect's plans for a building is a

    a) script   b) scantling   c) blueprint   d) mortise   20.___

The key is on page 203.   Possible score, 20   Your score _____

Section Twelve

FINAL TESTS

Read the directions for each of the subtests in this group. Then work rapidly without the aid of a dictionary or other reference.

Part A ◆ VOCATIONS AND INDUSTRIES

DIRECTIONS ◆ Indicate your answers by writing the letter on the blank at the right.

1. A business organization supplying gas and electricity to an area is known as

    a) a public utility   b) a brokerage   c) a trust company   1.___

2. A person learning an art or trade is

    a) a journeyman   b) a technician   c) an apprentice   2.___

3. One who fails to pay on time the money he owes is

    a) a felon   b) a defaulter   c) an absconder   3.___

4. The sole owner of a business is the

    a) manager   b) superintendent   c) proprietor   4.___

5. One's occupation, business, or trade is his

    a) vocation   b) avocation   c) heritage   5.___

6. A person given work and pay is an

    a) applicant   b) employee   c) employer   6.___

7. A detailed list of stock or articles on hand is

    a) an invoice   b) an inventory   c) a budget   7.___

8. The protection, development, and management of natural resources is known as

    a) silviculture   b) conservation   c) agriculture   8.___

9. A part payment is

    a) an installment   b) a promissory note   c) a debit   9.___

10. Engineers who design and supervise the construction of roads, harbors, airfields, bridges, and sewer systems are, essentially,

    a) ceramic engineers   b) chemical engineers   c) civil engineers   10.___

Go on to Part B.

Part B ◆ SPECIALISTS

DIRECTIONS ◆ Indicate your answers by writing the letter on the blank at the right.

1. Driver-salesman

   a) chauffeur   b) routeman   c) statistician   1.___

2. One who takes dictation, usually in shorthand, and transcribes the notes on a typewriter

   a) receptionist   b) typist   c) stenographer   2.___

3. The highest ranking representative sent by one country to another

   a) ambassador   b) consul   c) economist   3.___

4. Person trained in the science of atmosphere and the weather

   a) cardiologist   b) cartographer   c) meteorologist   4.___

5. Physician who specializes in the care of infants and children

   a) pediatrician   b) podiatrist   c) orthodontist   5.___

6. One who figures risks, rates, and premiums for insurance companies

   a) bookkeeper   b) teller   c) actuary   6.___

7. One who provides any of a variety of beauty services, such as manicures, haircuts, hairstyling

   a) cosmetologist   b) geologist   c) teletypist   7.___

8. One who buys and sells (e.g., real estate) for others

   a) clerk   b) mason   c) broker   8.___

9. Specialist trained to plan meals to help people recover or maintain good health

   a) restaurateur   b) nurse's aid   c) dietitian   9.___

10. Airline employee who coordinates flight schedules and operations within a given area

   a) copilot   b) pilot   c) dispatcher   10.___

Part C ✦ NOUNS FROM TOMORROW'S JOBS

DIRECTIONS ✦ Indicate your answers by writing the letter on the blank at the right.

1. Body of an airplane

   a) chassis   b) fuselage   c) propeller   1. ___

2. Shelter for housing aircraft

   a) hangar   b) garage   c) runway   2. ___

3. Device to stop bleeding by compressing a blood vessel

   a) antidote   b) tourniquet   c) anesthetic   3. ___

4. Grant of money, especially one made by the government

   a) subsidy   b) annuity   c) franchise   4. ___

5. Device for mixing air with gas to make an explosive mixture, as for an automobile engine

   a) exhaust   b) carburetor   c) air conditioner   5. ___

6. Act of paying out

   a) disbursement   b) transcription   c) audition   6. ___

7. Instrument in an aircraft to measure distance above the earth's surface

   a) speedometer   b) ignition   c) altimeter   7. ___

8. Guarantee or pledge

   a) warranty   b) premium   c) option   8. ___

9. The making of textiles, apparel, aircraft, wood products, machinery, and so on

   a) manufacture   b) exportation   c) licensing   9. ___

10. Something expected to produce a profit or income or both

    a) withdrawal   b) premium   c) investment   10. ___

Part D ◆ WORDS OFTEN CONFUSED

DIRECTIONS ◆ Write out the word of your choice on the blank. Save the short lines at right for scoring, later on.

1. A rule, a fundamental belief, or truth is a *principle/principal.*

   _____ 1.___

2. Truthfulness is *voracity/veracity.* _____ 2.___

3. Paper, envelopes, and other writing materials are known as *stationary/*

   stationery. _____ 3.___

4. To order, direct, or give advice is to *proscribe/prescribe.*

   _____ 4.___

5. One who takes the lead, such as in a school or in a business is the *principal/*

   principle. _____ 5.___

6. To condemn or prohibit is to *proscribe/prescribe.* _____ 6.___

7. To give advice is to *council/counsel.* _____ 7.___

8. New scientific knowledge is bound to *effect/affect* job requirements.

   _____ 8.___

9. The team had its full *compliment/complement* of outstanding athletes.

   _____ 9.___

10. One who leaves his country to settle in another is an *immigrant/emigrant* from

    his native land. _____ 10.___

Part E ◆ GETTING THE MEANING
FROM THE CONTEXT

DIRECTIONS ◆ Try to discover the meaning of the *italicized* word as it is used in each passage. Then write the meaning on the blank.

1. Celebrating his one hundredth birthday, a man in Melbourne attributed his *longevity* to his lifelong interest in sports.

   _____ 1.___

2. Unlike many other officials, he was a man of few words; he was known far and wide for his *reticence*.

_____ 2.___

3. No words passed between them. Their facial expressions gave *tacit* approval to the suggestion.

_____ 3.___

4. For this group of workers, the committee was not interested in houses rooted to the ground, like those of the past. It was the plan, rather, to construct *mobile* homes.

_____ 4.___

5. The script for the play is concise and to the point. The author has a *laconic* facility with dialogue.

_____ 5.___

6. It was agreed that neither party should take the lead in reporting the story; the announcements were to be made *simultaneously*.

_____ 6.___

7. Some critics accused the manager of waste and extravagance; others went to the opposite extreme and blamed him for his *parsimony*.

_____ 7.___

8. Impelled by *premonitions* of his death, he talked over his affairs with his lawyer and drew up a will.

_____ 8.___

9. There was no plan and no appointment. The meeting of the two was *fortuitous*.

_____ 9.___

10. The boys were as different as night and day. Mark had a selfish concern only for his own interests. Martin was the *altruist*.

_____ 10.___

11. Today psychologists are asking children to draw pictures of their friends and family members in action. These *kinetic* drawings often make clear the nature of the youngsters' problems.

_____ 11.___

12. The quiet delicacy and good taste of the music is seen by the experts as a retreat from the shockingly *blatant* environment in which it is written.

_____ 12. ___

13. For some months he has been trying to get his campaign under way. There has been no public announcement, no aboveboard request for funds. Yet he has gained sufficient backing to build up a *clandestine* operation equipped with radio transmitters and carried on by a thousand recruits.

_____ 13. ___

14. If the children in the neighborhood rode their bicycles over his lawn, he grew angry; when their noise disturbed him, he lost his temper and shouted at them. He was known for his *irascible* disposition.

_____ 14. ___

15. The play was a *perennial* success. Introduced in the 1920's, it remained on stage several years. Brought back in the 1940's, it flourished, and then, in the 1960's, it demonstrated once again its long lasting appeal.

_____ 15. ___

16. The disease, which often afflicts the young, is characterized by an uncontrolled *proliferation* of certain white blood cells, which gradually crowd out the vital red blood cells.

_____ 16. ___

17. The expression "widow woman" is *redundant*.

_____ 17. ___

18. A truck driver and a true believer in advertising slogans, Jim had no *qualms* when he bought the supposedly overhauled car. But then when he drove away with it, he discovered a flaw: the brakes failed.

_____ 18. ___

19. One researcher observed that bleeding is encouraged, not *inhibited*, if the ear lobe is chilled.

_____ 19. ___

20. The people worry deeply that hard times may reach them. "Our paychecks are bigger, but we take home less," says the mayor, *articulating* the town's major obsession.

_____ 20. ___

Part F ✦ ANALOGIES

DIRECTIONS ✦ In each series, note the relationship between the first two words. Then choose the two other words which have most nearly the same relationship. Fill in the blanks with their letters *in the same order of relationship.*

EXAMPLE ✦ cat : kitten : : ___c___ : ___e___

      a) tent   b) brake   c) calf   d) quiz   e) cow

The letters e and c point to the best choices and indicate the order of relationship. A cat is to a kitten as a cow is to a calf.

1. abrupt : gradual : : _____ : _____

      a) mobile   b) adjustable   c) immovable   d) new   e) early   1.___

2. physician : patient : : _____ : _____

      a) teacher   b) university   c) client   d) parent   e) lawyer   2.___

3. shortage : surfeit : : _____ : _____

      a) excess   b) top   c) dawn   d) total   e) lack   3.___

4. convene : assemble : : _____ : _____

      a) assess   b) prescribe   c) adjourn   d) censure   e) criticize   4.___

5. statue : sculptor : : _____ : _____

      a) costume   b) curtain   c) writer   d) painter   e) script   5.___

6. confer : conferee : : _____ : _____

      a) recur   b) trainee   c) employee   d) employ   e) recurrences   6.___

7. bizarre : bazaar : : _____ : _____

      a) night   b) morning   c) knight   d) day   e) knighthood   7.___

8. predict : future : : _____ : _____

      a) present   b) past   c) reminisce   d) foretell   e) forget   8.___

9. heart : cardiac : : _____ : _____

      a) spinal   b) pulmonary   c) dental   d) digestion   e) lungs   9.___

10. cattle : herd : : _____ : _____
   a) covey   b) swarm   c) drove   d) wolves   e) quail   10.___

11. soprano : female : : _____ : _____
   a) infant   b) contralto   c) male   d) tenor   e) bass   11.___

12. overt : secret : : _____ : _____
   a) cautious   b) rash   c) clever   d) coy   e) humorous   12.___

13. audible : inaudible : : _____ : _____
   a) gustatory   b) visual   c) credible   d) invisible   e) visible   13.___

14. biennial : biannual : : _____ : _____
   a) 16   b) 12   c) 8   d) 4   e) 18   14.___

15. quell : incite : : _____ : _____
   a) harangue   b) ignite   c) extinguish   d) blame   e) decide   15.___

16. word : dictionary : : _____ : _____
   a) library   b) gymnasium   c) book   d) swimming pool   e) vista   16.___

17. adroit : inept : : _____ : _____
   a) skillful   b) studious   c) ailing   d) disobedient   e) awkward   17.___

18. cow : bovine : : _____ : _____
   a) canine   b) lupine   c) snake   d) equine   e) wolf   18.___

19. tricycle : bicycle : : _____ : _____
   a) four   b) three   c) two   d) one   e) zero   19.___

20. boat : water : : _____ : _____
   a) automobile   b) airplane   c) exhaust   d) fuselage   e) air   20.___

21. principal : principle : : _____ : _____
   a) sign   b) order   c) telephone   d) right   e) write   21.___

22. skeptical : credulous : : _____ : _____
   a) covert   b) doubtful   c) late   d) overt   e) ambitious   22.___

23. copyright : book : : _____ : _____

    a) buyer   b) seller   c) patent   d) slogan   e) invention   23.___

24. Saturday : week : : _____ : _____

    a) day   b) calendar   c) year   d) late   e) October   24.___

25. peninsula : continent : : _____ : _____

    a) lake   b) mountain   c) ocean   d) bay   e) isthmus   25.___

Part G ◆ WORD PARTS

DIRECTIONS ◆ The list below includes words with common prefixes, roots, or suffixes. Look at each word part and the examples. Then write the meaning of the word part on the blank. Do not mark the short line at the right of each item. Save it for scoring later on.

Word Part	Examples	Meaning	
1. omni	omnivorous, omnibus	_____	1.___
2. post	postdate, postscript	_____	2.___
3. geo	geography, geology	_____	3.___
4. tele	telephone, telegraph	_____	4.___
5. auto	automotive, autograph	_____	5.___
6. inter	international, interfere	_____	6.___
7. sub	subway, submarine	_____	7.___
8. re	reclaim, renew	_____	8.___
9. chron	chronological, chronic	_____	9.___
10. bene	benefactor, beneficiary	_____	10.___
11. fore	foresight, forethought	_____	11.___
12. mono	monologue, monotone	_____	12.___
13. in	infirm, indecent, inactive	_____	13.___
14. fy, ify	magnify, fortify	_____	14.___
15. il	illegible, illegal	_____	15.___

16.	tran, trans	transport, transcribe	_____	16.__
17.	anti	antidote, antiseptic	_____	17.__
18.	hood	statehood, childhood	_____	18.__
19.	less	thoughtless, witless	_____	19.__
20.	ate	activate, animate	_____	20.__
21.	port	import, portable	_____	21.__
22.	arium, orium	auditorium, aquarium	_____	22.__
23.	vert, vers	revert, version	_____	23.__
24.	a, ab	atypical, abnormal	_____	24.__
25.	circum	circumnavigate	_____	25.__

Part H ◆ LISTING SYNONYMS AND ANTONYMS

1. Write five words that mean the same, or nearly the same, as *skillful*.

   _____   _____   _____

   _____   _____   1.__

2. Write five words that have the general meaning of *take*.

   _____   _____   _____

   _____   _____   2.__

3. Write five words with the same general meaning as *old*.

   _____   _____   _____

   _____   _____   3.__

4. Write five words with about the same meaning as *kind* (*gentle*).

   _____   _____   _____

   _____   _____   4.__

5. Write five words each meaning the opposite of *small*.

   _____   _____   _____

   _____   _____   5.__

Part I ◆ SPELLING

1. Change *liquid* into a verb meaning "to make liquid." _____   1. ___

2. Change *acquit* to a noun. _____   2. ___

3. Change *occur* to a noun. _____   3. ___

4. Write a word beginning with the letter *p* that means "at the same distance apart everywhere." _____   4. ___

5. Write a word beginning with the syllable *em* and meaning "disturb (a person), make self-conscious." _____   5. ___

6. Write a word beginning with the letter *g* and meaning "measure," or "to measure," or "an instrument for measuring." _____   6. ___

7. Write a word beginning with the letter *a* and meaning "one who does something for pleasure rather than for pay," or "one who does something rather poorly."

   _____   7. ___

8. Write a word beginning with *w* and meaning "unearthly, mysterious." "We were wakened by a _____ shriek."   8. ___

9. Write a verb beginning with the letter *p* and meaning "predict" or "foretell."

   _____   9. ___

10. Change *propel* to a noun meaning "a device that propels."

   _____   10. ___

Part J ◆ MEANINGS OF GENERAL WORDS

DIRECTIONS ◆ From each group below select the lettered word or phrase that most nearly corresponds in meaning to the *italicized* word. Write the letter on the blank at the right. Work rapidly.

1. *diffident* at times
   - a) fierce, savage
   - b) artistic, clever
   - c) misunderstood
   - d) shy, retiring   1. ___

2. with *therapeutic* value

    a) financial

    b) curative

    c) disciplinary

    d) literary

2. ___

3. to *convene*

    a) assemble

    b) defend

    c) recall

    d) make comfortable

3. ___

4. *sporadic* attacks

    a) wild, disorganized

    b) occurring now and then

    c) aerial

    d) political

4. ___

5. make a *memorandum*

    a) informal record

    b) debut

    c) great name

    d) recording machine

5. ___

6. no longer an *alien*

    a) foreigner

    b) minor

    c) chauffeur

    d) enemy

6. ___

7. no *tangible* effect

    a) harmful

    b) helpful

    c) real; definite

    d) curative

7. ___

8. known for his *mendacity*

    a) wealth

    b) habit of lying

    c) generosity

    d) physical strength

8. ___

9. to *lubricate* the machinery

    a) grease

    b) repair

    c) replace

    d) test

9. ___

10. usually *tractable*

    a) well mannered

    b) easy to deal with

    c) grammatical

    d) industrious

10. ___

11. neither acute nor *chronic*

    a) spread by contact

    b) long lasting

    c) very severe

    d) infectious

11. ___

12. not apt to *deteriorate*

   a) depart
   b) remember

   c) disagree
   d) grow worse

   12. ___

13. a powerful *adversary*

   a) opponent
   b) ruler

   c) athlete
   d) disciplinarian

   13. ___

14. occasional *insomnia*

   a) forgetfulness
   b) fear

   c) sleeplessness
   d) hysteria

   14. ___

15. regarded as a *novice*

   a) threat
   b) beginner

   c) expert
   d) colleague

   15. ___

16. began to *reminisce*

   a) grow better
   b) talk about the past

   c) stutter
   d) raise questions

   16. ___

17. with *covert* glances

   a) secret
   b) fearful

   c) friendly
   d) curious

   17. ___

18. demanding *suffrage*

   a) medical care
   b) pay increases

   c) the right to vote
   d) better housing

   18. ___

19. an admirable *principal*

   a) fundamental belief
   b) general plan

   c) chief person
   d) policy

   19. ___

20. always *voracious*

   a) ravenous
   b) quarrelsome

   c) mysterious
   d) wholesome

   20. ___

21. a *bucolic* life

   a) monotonous
   b) physically active

   c) pastoral; rustic
   d) well planned

   21. ___

22. known as a *gregarious* person

    a) fond of being with
       other people
    b) eager to learn

    c) sports loving
    d) talkative

22.___

23. a *precarious* undertaking

    a) costly
    b) strange, grotesque

    c) courageous
    d) risky

23.___

24. a *diminutive* creature

    a) untamed, wild
    b) tiny

    c) self-satisfied
    d) industrious

24.___

25. *adamant* in his stand

    a) unyielding
    b) unfair

    c) pompous
    d) prejudiced

25.___

26. with a *pessimistic* prediction

    a) gloomy
    b) secret

    c) light-hearted
    d) stupid

26.___

27. and no *bouillon*

    a) thin, clear soup
    b) bars of gold or silver

    c) currency
    d) mayonnaise

27.___

28. the *overbearing* attitude

    a) pastoral, rural
    b) urban

    c) domineering
    d) penitent

28.___

29. a *cardiac* condition

    a) abnormal
    b) heart

    c) painful
    d) abdominal

29.___

30. a *symptom* to be watched

    a) performer
    b) sign, indication

    c) program
    d) political candidate

30.___

31. receive a *dividend*

    a) announcement
    b) advertisement

    c) receipt
    d) share of the profits

31.___

32. down the *runway*

   a) exercise field
   b) leakage

   c) landing strip for planes
   d) plane with two wings

   32.___

33. with *negotiable* assets

   a) of doubtful worth
   b) valuable

   c) additional
   d) transferable

   33.___

34. searching for an *antidote*

   a) remedy
   b) fortune

   c) lost mine
   d) pain reliever

   34.___

35. to provide *collateral*

   a) proof
   b) additional security

   c) payment
   d) money lent at interest

   35.___

36. to take a *census*

   a) numbering of the population
   b) account of assets

   c) vote
   d) sampling

   36.___

37. become a *lessee*

   a) person to whom a lease is
      granted
   b) beneficiary

   c) purchaser
   d) guarantor

   37.___

38. usually *taciturn*

   a) resentful
   b) unwilling to talk

   c) buoyant
   d) cooperative

   38.___

39. *eligible* to take the position

   a) eager
   b) unwilling

   c) qualified
   d) unprepared

   39.___

40. a *versatile* genius

   a) conceited
   b) mathematical

   c) conversational
   d) many-sided

   40.___

41. equipped with a *semaphore*

   a) typewriter
   b) apparatus for signaling

   c) carburetor
   d) brake

   41.___

42. speak to the *proprietor*

    a) owner
    b) manager
    c) actuary
    d) beneficiary

42. ___

43. and *reimburse* him

    a) inform
    b) thank
    c) patronize
    d) repay

43. ___

44. *superfluous* words

    a) descriptive
    b) coined on the moment
    c) persuasive
    d) needless

44. ___

45. to *maneuver* the car

    a) mortgage
    b) repair
    c) purchase
    d) operate skillfully

45. ___

46. to *placate* the customer

    a) repay
    b) compliment
    c) soothe the anger of
    d) promise

46. ___

47. to their *habitat*

    a) customary diet
    b) dwelling place
    c) riding costume
    d) conference

47. ___

48. *ingenuous* remarks

    a) clever, witty
    b) satirical
    c) simple, innocent
    d) discourteous

48. ___

49. an *archaic* word

    a) colorful
    b) technical
    c) confusing
    d) no longer in use

49. ___

50. hire a *craftsman*

    a) skilled workman
    b) apprentice
    c) foreman
    d) contractor

50. ___

The key is on page 204.

Part		Possible score	Your score
A	Vocations and Industries	10	_____
B	Specialists	10	_____
C	Nouns from Tomorrow's Jobs	10	_____
D	Words Often Confused	10	_____
E	Getting the Meaning from Context	20	_____
F	Analogies	25	_____
G	Word Parts	25	_____
H	Listing Synonyms and Antonyms	25	_____
I	Spelling	10	_____
J	Meanings of General Words	50	_____
	Total	195	_____

APPRAISAL OF PROGRESS

It has been the purpose of this book to help you extend and enrich your vocabulary, build your spelling competence, and develop effective methods of word approach and word usage. To what extent have you succeeded in "breaking the word barrier"?

Begin your appraisal by comparing your scores on the tests in Section Twelve with those of Section One. In addition, study your scores on the exercises in the book and analyze the trends for different types of drills. Finally, give special attention to your independent work. Wherever the scores or your personal judgment indicate that you have made an important gain, place a plus mark on the appropriate blank at the right.

CHECK LIST

Important gains

1. Alertness to strange words of importance to you

   a) Terms from your occupational field _____

   b) Other occupational terms _____

   c) General words _____

   d) Whimsical words _____

2. Effectiveness in arriving independently at meanings

   a) Through context clues _____

   b) Through word parts _____

3. Use of the dictionary

   a) For checking inferences _____

   b) For learning acceptable pronunciations _____

   c) For checking spellings _____

   d) For looking up multiple meanings _____

4. Adoption of a systematic plan for adding words to your active vocabulary

   a) Recording the data on cards _____

   b) Reciting from memory _____

   c) Checking _____

   d) Using the new words _____

5. Knowledge of meanings

   a) Words in the book _____

   b) Others _____

6. Knowledge of word parts

   a) Those in the book _____

   b) Others _____

7. Sharpening and refining knowledge of words already partly familiar

   a) Formulating definitions _____

   b) Listing antonyms and synonyns _____

   c) Considering multiple meanings _____

   d) Seeking to specify—to select the best word to express a particular meaning _____

8. Tackling spelling demons effectively

    a) By viewing the word as a whole or in large units   _____

    b) By focusing attention on hard spots   _____

    c) By making aggressive efforts to recall   _____

    d) By correcting mistakes immediately through new study   _____

    e) By reviewing frequently   _____

9. Interest in words   _____

Now write a brief statement regarding your progress. Have you a strong and continuing interest in words? Do you tend to grasp readily the meanings of strange words? Do you keep your vocabulary viable so that it grows and expands as your needs and interests develop?

In writing and speaking, do you direct attention to the choice of suitable words? Have you a systematic plan for learning the spelling of troublesome words?

PERSONAL APPRAISAL

Keys

NOTE: If any answer of yours is different from the one given in the key, and you think you are correct, check with your dictionary. Give yourself credit, if credit is due.

Section one

Part A ◆ Vocations and Industries, p. 3

1. a   2. c   3. b   4. c   5. a   6. b   7. b   8. b   9. a   10. c

Part B ◆ Specialists, p. 4

1. b   2. c   3. a   4. c   5. a   6. c   7. a   8. c   9. c   10. c

Part C ◆ Nouns from Tomorrow's Jobs, p. 4

1. b   2. a   3. b   4. a   5. b   6. a   7. c   8. a   9. a   10. c

Part D ◆ Words Often Confused, p. 5

1. principle	3. stationery	5. principal	7. counsel	9. complement
2. veracity	4. prescribe	6. proscribe	8. affect	10. emigrant

Part E ◆ Getting the Meaning from the Context, pp. 6–7

1. long life
2. tendency to say little
3. implied or understood without being openly expressed
4. movable; easily moved
5. concise
6. at the same time; together
7. stinginess; extreme economy
8. forewarnings
9. accidental; happening by chance
10. unselfish person; one concerned with the welfare of others
11. of motion
12. noisy, loud-mouthed, or showy
13. secret, concealed
14. irritable; easily made angry
15. enduring; lasting a long time; lasting through the years
16. rapid and repeated production
17. using too many words for the same idea
18. misgivings; doubts
19. checked; restrained
20. enunciating; putting into words

Part F ◆ Analogies, pp. 8–9

1. a:c or c:a	6. d:c	11. d:c	16. c:a	21. d:e or e:d
2. e:c	7. a:c or c:a	12. a:b or b:a	17. a:e	22. a:d or d:a
3. e:a	8. c:b	13. e:d	18. e:b	23. c:e
4. d:e or e:d	9. e:b	14. a:d	19. b:c	24. e:c
5. e:c	10. e:a	15. c:b	20. b:e	25. d:c

Part G ◆ Word Parts, p. 10

1. all	10. well	18. state of, condition of
2. after	11. beforehand	19. without
3. earth	12. one	20. make, cause to be
4. distant	13. not	21. carry
5. self	14. make, cause to be	22. place for
6. between	15. not	23. turn
7. under	16. across, over	24. not, away from
8. back, again, back again	17. against	25. around
9. time		

Part H ◆ Listing Synonyms and Antonyms, p. 11

1. Any 5: adept, adroit, deft, clever, apt, proficient, dexterous

2. Any 5: accept, receive, get, steal, pocket, gather, snatch, abduct

3. Any 5: ancient, venerable, antique, archaic, obsolete, aged

4. Any 5: benign, generous, good, humane, forbearing, obliging, friendly

5. Any 5: big, huge, enormous, significant, great, large, massive, vast, immense

Part I ◆ Spelling, pp. 11–12

1. liquefy	3. occurrence	5. embarrass	7. amateur	9. prophesy
2. acquittal	4. parallel	6. gauge	8. weird	10. propeller

Part J ◆ Meanings of General Words, pp. 12–16

1. d	6. a	11. b	16. b	21. c	26. a	31. d	36. a	41. b	46. c
2. b	7. c	12. d	17. a	22. a	27. a	32. c	37. a	42. a	47. b
3. a	8. b	13. a	18. c	23. d	28. c	33. d	38. b	43. d	48. c
4. b	9. a	14. c	19. c	24. b	29. b	34. a	39. c	44. d	49. d
5. a	10. b	15. b	20. a	25. a	30. b	35. b	40. d	45. d	50. a

NOTE: If any answer of yours is different from the one given in the key, and you think you are correct, check with your dictionary. Give yourself credit, if credit is due.

Section two

Exercise 1 ◆ Adapting Word Forms, pp. 25–26

1. abruptly
2. taciturnity
3. intractable
4. reminiscences
5. skeptic
6. carnivore
7. decrepitude
8. dissension
9. audacious
10. vindication

Exercise 2 ◆ Finding Antonyms, p. 26

1. b   2. d   3. c   4. d   5. a   6. a   7. d   8. d

Exercise 3 ◆ Writing Homonyms, p. 27

1. wait   2. peace   3. whole   4. principal   5. waist   6. plane   7. hour   8. residents

Exercise 4 ◆ Finding Synonyms, p. 27

1. b   2. d   3. d   4. a   5. c   6. a   7. a   8. c

Exercise 5 ◆ Writing Synonyms, p. 28

1. mistake, blunder
2. hoard, rescue, retain, keep
3. receive, take (adopt)
4. approve, compliment, praise
5. tour, trip, jaunt
6. power, vigor, force
7. maintain, hold, detain, retain, reserve
8. spread, disseminate
9. endurance, forbearance
10. timidity, apprehensiveness, dread, alarm, fright, dismay

Exercise 6 ◆ Writing Antonyms, p. 28

1. rash, careless, slovenly
2. refuse, reject, decline
3. happiness, pleasure, cheer, joy
4. robust, hardy, tough
5. actual, real, existent
6. hasten, hurry, speed
7. reward, recompense
8. fall, sink, decrease
9. sweet, saccharine, honeyed, sugary
10. loosen, relax, slacken

NOTE: If you have written other answers and think you are correct, check your responses with the dictionary.

Exercise 7 ◆ Getting the Meaning from the Context, pp. 29–31

1. a flowing in; steady flow
2. apparent self-contradiction, or statement that may be true, but seems to say two opposite things
3. inequality; difference
4. possibility of two or more meanings
5. crime of setting fire to property
6. relating to a violent change, such as a flood, earthquake, or war
7. complete difference; unlikeness
8. reputation, influence, or distinction based upon what is known of one's ability and achievements
9. increased; enlarged
10. self-governing; independent
11. having to do with land, its use, or its ownership
12. stealthy; secret
13. possible as opposed to actual; capable of coming into being
14. matter that settles to the bottom of a liquid
15. reward; pay; payment

Exercise 8 ◆ Analogies, pp. 31–32

1. dexterity
2. prefix
3. lethal
4. affluent
5. audacity
6. anecdote
7. elated
8. reminiscence
9. entice
10. novice
11. asset
12. upright
13. extinguish
14. cupidity
15. fortitude

Exercise 9 ◆ Review, pp. 32–33

1. d
2. c
3. a
4. b
5. b
6. b
7. a
8. b
9. c
10. d
11. a
12. c
13. b
14. a or c
15. a

Section three

Exercise 10 ◆ Identifying Meanings through Word Parts, pp. 35–36

1. b 2. d 3. a 4. c 5. d 6. b 7. d 8. d 9. c 10. d

Exercise 11 ◆ Supplying the Words Defined, p. 36

1. transcribe
2. preeminent
3. transplant
4. omnivorous
5. submerge
6. misbehavior
7. exhale; expire
8. subnormal

Exercise 12 ◆ Supplying Words with the Prefixes Provided, p. 37

1. Any 3: prepare, prevent, precede, prefabricated, preview, prehistoric, premature
2. Any 3: misguided, mistrust, misinformed, misfortune, mismanaged, mishandled, misunderstanding
3. Any 3: transport, transmit, transpose, transfer, transparent, translucent

NOTE: If you have written other words and think you are correct, consult your dictionary.

Exercise 13 ◆ Speed of Interpretation, pp. 42–43

Column 1: 4, 5, 8, 13, 14, 18, 20, 21, 24, 28, 32, 35, 37
Column 2: 2, 6, 7, 10, 12, 13, 18, 23, 24, 25, 29, 30, 32, 33, 36, 39, 40

Exercise 14 ◆ Changing Word Forms, pp. 45–46

1. allergic
2. asphyxiation
3. insomniac
4. malnourished
5. contagion
6. therapists
7. chronicle
8. fatal
9. somnambulist
10. therapy

Exercise 15 ◆ Matching Words and Meanings, p. 46

1. e   2. g   3. a   4. c   5. b

Exercise 16 ◆ Matching Words and Meanings, p. 47

1. d   2. f   3. g   4. h   5. b

Exercise 17 ◆ Matching Words and Meanings, p. 47

1. f   2. g   3. h   4. d   5. a

Exercise 18 ◆ Words Often Confused, p. 48

1. complement
2. imminent
3. biannual; biennial
4. confidant
5. compliment
6. confident
7. eminent
8. ingenious
9. ingenuous
10. overt
11. complement
12. covert

Section four

Exercise 19 ◆ Discovering Word Meanings Through Context Clues, pp. 51–52

1. offhand; spoken or done without preparation
2. pay back
3. agree; be of the same opinion
4. winding, crooked; full of twists and bends
5. meantime; time in between
6. using two languages
7. opening; gap
8. systematic effort to spread opinions or beliefs
9. taking place in or on the water
10. implied or understood without being openly expressed
11. cheery, mirthful, lively
12. truthfulness
13. involving death
14. abrupt, rapid, quick
15. pleasant features

Exercise 20 ◆ Noting Varied Meanings of Everyday Words, p. 53

1. Any 3: solid piece of metal, wood, stone; obstruct, hinder; part of a city enclosed by streets; group of things of the same kind

2. Any 3: piece of timber, etc., used as a support; fasten (a notice); place where a soldier is stationed; job or position; mail

3. Any 3: final; endure; block shaped like a foot; next before the present (as last week)

4. Any 3: piece of cloth that represents a country, state, group, and so on; signal (as flag a train); droop, grow weak; flower (iris)

5. Any 3: current of air; plan, sketch; selection of persons for a special purpose; act of pulling loads

NOTE: For other meanings, consult your dictionary.

Exercise 21 ◆ Changing Word Forms, p. 55

1. convention
2. subsidize
3. eloquence
4. stable
5. disfranchise
6. disburse
7. tenant
8. mendacious
9. annually
10. exuberance

Exercise 22 ◆ Matching Words and Definitions, pp. 55–56

1. f	1. c
2. e	2. f
3. a	3. a
4. c	4. h
5. g	5. g

Exercise 23 ◆ Directive Words Used in Essay Examination Questions, pp. 56–58

1. define	4. contrast	7. describe	10. explain
2. enumerate	5. enumerate	8. evaluate	11. define
3. justify	6. compare	9. summarize	12. trace

Exercise 24 ◆ Seeing Relationships, pp. 58–59

1. c	3. d	5. d	7. d	9. d	11. d	13. e	15. d	17. d	19. d
2. e	4. a	6. e	8. c	10. a	12. a	14. d	16. c	18. b	20. c

Exercise 25 ◆ Seeing Relationships, p. 59

1. c	3. b	5. c	7. d	9. c	11. d	13. c	15. c	17. b	19. c
2. e	4. b	6. a	8. b	10. e	12. d	14. b	16. a	18. d	20. d

Exercise 26 ◆ Writing the Required Word, p. 60

1. interurban	6. rehabilitate	11. polyglot
2. intrastate	7. interim, intermission	12. autograph
3. polytechnic	8. intermingled, interwoven	13. return, revert
4. predict	9. automotive, automatic	14. supernatural
5. superman	10. international	15. reimburse, remit

Exercise 27 ◆ Review, pp. 61–62

1. d	4. b	7. d	10. d	13. a
2. a	5. a	8. a	11. c	14. b
3. d	6. c	9. b	12. c	15. c

Exercise 28 ◆ Recall, pp. 62–63

1. default	3. franchise	5. therapeutic	7. transfusion
2. subsidize	4. commission	6. concussion	8. sporadic

NOTE: An answer is correct only if the word is *chosen and spelled* correctly.

Section five

Exercise 29 ◆ Judging the Definition, p. 66

1. X;   2. N;   3. N;   4. M

Exercise 30 ◆ Definition, p. 66

A football stadium is an oval structure around an enclosed playing field. It is usually made up of terraced elevations with tiers of seats for the spectators.

Exercise 31 ◆ Finding Antonyms, p. 67

1. b	3. a	5. a	7. c	9. a	11. a	13. d	15. b	17. a	19. d
2. c	4. c	6. b	8. a	10. c	12. b	14. b	16. d	18. a	20. c

Exercise 32 ◆ Finding Synonyms, p. 68

1. b	3. b	5. d	7. c	9. c	11. d	13. b	15. a	17. b	19. a
2. c	4. a	6. b	8. d	10. a or b	12. b	14. b	16. d	18. c	20. c

Exercise 33 ◆ Arriving at Meanings through Context Clues, pp. 70–71

1. excused; overlooked
2. one who watches without taking part
3. command; order
4. died
5. agree
6. stinginess; extreme economy
7. declining; decreasing
8. brief stay; visit
9. position requiring little work and usually paying well
10. profitable; bringing in money
11. forbidden; banned; prohibited
12. persons who do something bad or foolish
13. tiny living creature
14. higher position or rank
15. branched off

Exercise 34 ◆ Seeing the Meanings of Word Parts, pp. 72–73

1. c	6. b	11. a
2. d	7. a	12. b
3. a	8. a	13. d
4. b	9. c	14. a
5. c	10. b	15. c

Exercise 35 ◆ Speed of Interpretation, p. 74

Column 1: 3, 4, 6, 9, 14, 15, 16, 17, 21, 23, 24, 27, 30, 31, 32, 36, 40

Column 2: 4, 5, 11, 12, 13, 15, 16, 18, 21, 24, 25, 29, 33, 34, 38, 39, 40

Exercise 36 ◆ Speed of Interpretation, p. 75

Column 1: 2, 3, 4, 6, 12, 13, 14, 19, 20, 23, 26, 27, 31, 34, 36, 38

Column 2: 1, 3, 6, 7, 8, 9, 13, 15, 16, 19, 22, 24, 27, 28, 30, 35, 36, 37, 38, 39, 40

Exercise 37 ◆ Review, pp. 76–77

1. antonym	7. commission	13. novice	19. habitat	25. cavalcade
2. asphyxiate	8. taciturn	14. exotic	20. adamant	26. anesthetic
3. carnivorous	9. default	15. broker	21. malignant	27. tangible
4. therapeutic	10. allergy	16. subsidy	22. clientele	28. synonym
5. franchise	11. concussion	17. antidote	23. fatality	29. covert
6. mendacity	12. ingenuous	18. diffident	24. confidant	30. tractable

Section six

Exercise 38 ◆ Changing Word Forms, pp. 80–81

1. acquittal	4. vigilance	7. solicitor	10. counsel
2. revoke	5. enigmatic	8. diurnal	11. statute
3. migrate	6. arsonist	9. potentate	12. dessert

Exercise 39 ◆ Framing a Definition, p. 82

Read the four "definitions" that follow, and note the rating for each. Then judge the definition you wrote. Place an X beside it if you rate it as satisfactory, an N to indicate that it is too narrow, a B to indicate that it is too broad, or M if it is a misstatement.

1. Rationalization is the criminal, defensive reaction of an individual accused of a crime. 1. M

2. Rationalization is a way of buttressing self-esteem by giving creditable reasons for behavior or beliefs that we do not regard as worthy. There are several forms: belittling something we wanted and did not get, trying to convince ourselves that what we have is best, or blaming other people or things for our own failures and frustrations. 2. X

3. Rationalization is a "sour grapes" reaction. Like the fox who wanted a certain bunch of grapes but couldn't reach it and then declared he didn't want it because it was sour, we sometimes try for something and then if we fail to get it, belittle it.   3. N

4. Rationalization is man's way of buttressing self-esteem.   4. B

Exercise 40   ◆   Word Usage, p. 82

1. procession
2. parade (or promenade)
3. file
4. cavalcade
5. pageant
6. parade
7. pilgrimage
8. cortege

Exercise 41   ◆   Word Usage, p. 83

1. inquire
2. lecture
3. debate
4. rant
5. recite
6. converse
7. chatter
8. answer

Exercise 42   ◆   Word Usage, p. 83

1. zephyr
2. blizzard
3. gust
4. tornado (or whirlwind)
5. gale
6. hurricane (or cyclone)

Exercise 43   ◆   Framing a Definition, p. 83

1. roughly built hut or cabin
2. large, stately house
3. small house, often a small house at a summer resort
4. apartment or house on the top of another building

NOTE: If your reply to any of these questions on definitions or usage differs from the one given in the key, consult your dictionary. Give yourself credit if you can support your stand.

Exercise 44   ◆   Completing Analogies, p. 84

1. defeated
2. flooded
3. covey
4. contralto
5. amateur
6. fracture
7. carnivore
8. mathematics
9. vocation
10. preface
11. provender
12. glacier
13. liability
14. malicious
15. sedan
16. banquet

Exercise 45   ◆   Making Use of Prefix Knowledge, pp. 85–86

1. d
2. c
3. a
4. c
5. a
6. a
7. b
8. d
9. c
10. a
11. d
12. b
13. a
14. d
15. c

Exercise 46 ◆ Choosing the Better Word, pp. 86–88

1. council	6. roll	11. ordinance	16. canvass	21. hue
2. eminent	7. overt	12. effect	17. confident	22. ingenious
3. brake	8. biennial	13. sensory	18. stature	23. attendants
4. corps	9. principal	14. impassable	19. capital	24. horde
5. diary	10. recipe	15. illegible	20. inert	25. disease

Exercise 47 ◆ Spotting Superfluous Words, pp. 88–89

1. woman	8. still	15. in advance	24. upward
3. in the morning	9. under the water	17. self-centered	25. made after death
5. ahead of time	11. puzzling	18. present	
6. made once a year	14. between cities	20. at the present time	

Exercise 48 ◆ The Meanings of Common Word Parts, p. 89

1. distant, far, far off	4. inflammation of	7. under	9. not
2. not	5. in advance, before	8. study of, knowledge of, science of	10. with, together
3. make, cause to be	6. over, across		

Exercise 49 ◆ Review, pp. 90–91

Part A	Part B	Part C	Part D	Part E	Part F
1. g	1. h	1. f	1. f	1. c	1. e
2. e	2. f	2. d	2. e	2. e	2. c
3. a	3. d	3. e	3. a	3. f	3. a
4. b	4. a	4. a	4. c	4. a	4. d
5. c	5. e	5. b	5. g	5. b	5. b

Section seven

Exercise 50 ◆ Changing Word Forms, p. 96

1. metropolis	3. consulate	5. maintain	7. reclaimed	9. judiciary
2. alienate	4. legislator	6. ineligible	8. naturalization	10. franchise

Exercise 51 ◆ Words Ending in "ology," p. 97

1. meteorology   2. criminology   3. geology   4. zoology   5. psychology

Exercise 52 ◆ Supplying the Missing Word, pp. 97–99

1. draftsmen	6. surveyors	11. sentient, sensing
2. redeemed	7. tourniquet	12. indispensable
3. millwrights	8. exodus or departure	13. civil engineers
4. criteria	9. psychologists	14. portability
5. naturalization	10. carpenters	15. precipitation

NOTE: If any answer differs from the one in the key, and you think you are correct, check with your dictionary.

Exercise 53 ◆ Speed of Comprehension, p. 100

1. c	3. b	5. b	7. a	9. d	11. a	13. c	15. d	17. e	19. c
2. d	4. a	6. c	8. e	10. a	12. c	14. d	16. d	18. c	20. a

Exercise 54 ◆ Speed of Comprehension, p. 101

1. c	3. d	5. e	7. d	9. e	11. a	13. a	15. a	17. c	19. a
2. b	4. b	6. a	8. b	10. c	12. a	14. b	16. e	18. a	20. a

Exercise 55 ◆ Analogies, pp. 102–3

1. e:a	5. e:d	9. d:b	13. a:d	17. e:c
2. b:d or d:b	6. a:e	10. e:d	14. c:d	18. d:e
3. e:c	7. c:d	11. a:b or b:a	15. e:b	19. d:b
4. d:a	8. a:b or b:a	12. e:c	16. b:c or c:b	20. e:c

Exercise 56 ◆ Selecting the Most Suitable Word, p. 104

1. overbearing	3. demure	5. gullible	7. morose	9. eminent
2. versatile	4. nonchalant	6. boisterous	8. miserly	10. mute

Exercise 57 ◆ Selecting the Most Suitable Word, p. 105

1. concurred   2. reimbursed   3. subsidized   4. deteriorated   5. dissented

Exercise 58 ◆ Getting the Meaning from the Context, pp. 105–6

1. fixed money charge for the use of a highway, for example, or a bridge or waterway

2. wipe out, destroy, make meaningless

3. those who copy (money) in order to deceive or defraud

4. change (a law, bill, motion)

5. disperse, dissolve

6. series of related activities planned for a particular purpose

7. confirm; approve

8. financial, having to do with the treasury or the exchequer

9. make a statement under oath to prove that something is true

10. government grant to a person stating that he is the only one allowed to make or sell a certain invention for a certain number of years

11. tax on the manufacture, sale, or use of certain articles made or sold within a country

12. expert in matters relating to the production, distribution, and consumption of wealth

Exercise 59 ◆ Review, pp. 107–8

Part A	Part B	Part C	Part D	Part E
1. c	1. g	1. e	1. g	1. h
2. f	2. b	2. d	2. f	2. f
3. b	3. a	3. a	3. a	3. a
4. d	4. f	4. c	4. e	4. d
5. e	5. c	5. b	5. d	5. e

Section eight

Exercise 60 ◆ Key Words in Essay Examination Questions, pp. 110–11

1. enumerate (or list)   3. trace   5. contrast   7. explain   9. justify
2. summarize   4. define   6. illustrate   8. compare   10. discuss

Exercise 61 ◆ Words Often Confused, p. 111

1. emerged   2. prophecy   3. principle   4. diffident   5. affect

Exercise 62 ◆ Supplying the Required Words, p. 113

1. insolvent   4. proprietor   7. indorsement,   8. lien
2. invest   5. testator   endorsement,   9. currency
3. overdraft   6. usury   or signature   10. collateral

Exercise 63 ◆ Writing Antonyms and Synonyms, p. 113

Antonyms

1. inconvenient
2. unprofitable
3. cultivated, civilized, tame, gentle, or mild
4. false, spurious, or artificial
5. valueless or worthless

Synonyms

1. truthfulness
2. penniless, poverty-stricken, or impecunious
3. fierce, savage, turbulent, stormy, or tempestuous
4. dead or deceased
5. blame, censure, reproach, or scold

Exercise 64 ◆ Common Word Parts, pp. 114–15

1. b   2. d   3. a   4. c   5. c   6. a   7. a   8. a   9. d   10. c

Exercise 65 ◆ Writing the Required Word, pp. 115–16

1. semiannual or semiannually
2. respond
3. irreversible
4. convention
5. panacea
6. semiweekly
7. retract
8. autobiography
9. discourtesy
10. superintend or supervise

Exercise 66 ◆ Selecting the Required Word, pp. 116–17

1. hike
2. trudge
3. prowl
4. stalk
5. patrol
6. wander
7. promenade
8. stride
9. march
10. toddle

Exercise 67 ◆ Selecting the Required Word, p. 117

1. shoal   2. litter (or farrow)   3. covey   4. swarm   5. pack   6. flight

Exercise 68 ◆ Selecting the Suitable Word, p. 117

1. pretty or beautiful
2. graceful
3. magnificent
4. handsome
5. gorgeous
6. exquisite

Exercise 69 ◆ Finding Antonyms, p. 118

1. c   3. a   5. a   7. a   9. a   11. d   13. d   15. d   17. c   19. c
2. b   4. c   6. d   8. d   10. b   12. a   14. c   16. c   18. a   20. b

Exercise 70 ◆ *Finding Homonyms, p. 119*

1. c	3. c	5. b	7. c	9. c	11. a	13. d	15. c	17. a	19. c
2. d	4. a	6. d	8. b	10. d	12. b	14. a	16. d	18. b	20. a

Exercise 71 ◆ *Finding Synonyms, p. 120*

1. d	3. b	5. a	7. a	9. a	11. a	13. d	15. c	17. d	19. c
2. a	4. c	6. c	8. c	10. d	12. c	14. b	16. b	18. a	20. d

Exercise 72 ◆ *Recall, pp. 121–22*

1. usury
2. inventory
3. collateral
4. defaulting
5. contraband
6. currency
7. lien
8. franchise
9. brokerage
10. insolvent
11. tenant
12. deficit
13. larceny
14. dividends
15. draft

Section nine

Exercise 73 ◆ *Completing Analogies, pp. 125–26*

1. slander
2. dexterity or deftness
3. predict, foresee, or prognosticate
4. principle
5. lupine
6. therapy
7. decade
8. hangar
9. triplicate
10. tolerate
11. humility or humiliation
12. adversary or opponent
13. convene or assemble
14. taciturn
15. currency or money
16. metropolis or city
17. soap or water
18. dialogue
19. debit
20. meteorology

Exercise 74 ◆ *Important Word Parts, p. 126*

1. move
2. move
3. hold
4. write
5. written
6. send
7. draw, pull, take
8. carry
9. word
10. dip, plunge
11. breathe
12. see
13. to be alive
14. call, say, speak, tell
15. life
16. earth
17. hand
18. feel
19. citizen, citizenship
20. year

Exercise 75 ◆ Speed of Interpretation, p. 127

Column 1:   2, 7, 8, 9, 18, 21, 23, 25, 26, 32, 34, 36, 38, 39, 40

Column 2:   3, 5, 9, 11, 12, 13, 14, 15, 16, 22, 24, 25, 27, 30, 35, 36, 37, 39

Exercise 76 ◆ Speed of Interpretation, p. 128

Column 1:   2, 4, 5, 8, 10, 11, 15, 18, 21, 24, 25, 28, 29, 30, 33, 34, 35, 38, 39

Column 2:   1, 2, 3, 8, 11, 12, 14, 15, 20, 24, 25, 26, 29, 30, 31, 32, 33, 34, 35, 37, 38, 40

Exercise 77 ◆ Determining Meanings Through Word Parts, pp. 129–30

1. c	4. a	7. d	10. d	13. c
2. c	5. b	8. c	11. d	14. a
3. d	6. b	9. b	12. c	15. b

Exercise 78 ◆ Writing Suitable Adjectives and Nouns, pp. 130–31

Part A: (Any 4) pretty, lovely, fair, dainty, exquisite, bonny, beautiful

Part B: (Any 4) grotesque, odd, quaint, queer, peculiar, unconventional

Part C: (Any 4) trader, broker, dealer, monger, salesman, tradesman, retailer

NOTE: If your answer is not included in the key and you think you are correct, check with your dictionary.

Exercise 79 ◆ Getting the Meaning From the Context, pp. 131–32

1. long period of dry weather
2. lower the pride, dignity, or self-respect of
3. having to do with actors and acting
4. queer, unnatural, odd
5. fond of being with others
6. talking much about trifles
7. assumed names
8. hobby; something other than regular business that occupies a person's attention
9. plunder
10. incapable of being appeased
11. capable of being touched
12. pastoral, rustic, rural
13. freedom from punishment
14. position of the feet of a player, as when playing golf
15. with extreme or excessive care for details

Exercise 80 ◆ Review: Part A, pp. 133–34

1. d   2. c   3. a   4. d   5. c   6. d   7. a   8. a   9. b   10. d   11. a   12. c

Exercise 81 ◆ Review: Part B, pp. 134–35

1. c   2. c   3. b   4. a   5. b   6. d   7. c   8. c   9. a   10. d   11. a   12. d

Section ten

Exercise 82 ◆ Superfluous Words, pp. 138–39

1. no longer operating (or defunct)
2. of great age (or prehistoric)
5. at the same time (or simultaneous)
6. resulting in death (or fatal)
9. of his life
11. accurate
12. ahead of time
13. under the skin
18. that wavers (or vacillating)
20. made after death
22. afterwards
23. victorious
24. lunar (or of the moon)

Exercise 83 ◆ Nonobjective Expressions, p. 139

Column 1:   4, 6, 8, 9, 10, 11, 15, 16, 17, 18, 19, 20
Column 2:   3, 4, 5, 7, 8, 9, 11, 15, 16, 17, 20

Exercise 84 ◆ Meanings of Word Parts, p. 140

1. early, beforehand
2. back, again, or back again
3. not
4. with
5. against
6. absence of
7. carry
8. sent
9. between
10. over, across
11. write
12. time
13. under
14. say, speak, or tell
15. fake or false
16. again, back again
17. many
18. backward
19. not
20. with
21. one
22. out, out of
23. all
24. self
25. not

Exercise 85 ◆ Getting the Meaning from the Context, pp. 141–42

1. weak point; weakness
2. plan for travel, or route for travel
3. said in fun; jocose, or not to be taken seriously
4. hater of mankind; person who dislikes or mistrusts others
5. indirectly, not firsthand; through the experience of others
6. hardened, accustomed
7. the broad mouth of a river into which the tide flows; inlet from the sea
8. active, forceful, energetic
9. no longer in use; out of date
10. sluggish, dull, inactive

Exercise 86 ◆ Selecting the Suitable Word, p. 142

1. plagiarize
2. burgle
3. kidnap
4. swindle
5. ransack
6. loot
7. shoplift
8. pilfer

Exercise 87 ◆ Selecting the Suitable Word, p. 143

1. scenario
2. novel
3. fable
4. journal
5. comedy
6. autobiography
7. chronicle
8. satire

Exercise 88 ◆ Selecting the Suitable Word, p. 143

1. reaper   2. granary   3. incubator   4. fodder   5. prairie   6. mulch

Exercise 89 ◆ Selecting Antonyms, p. 144

1. b   2. a   3. c   4. c   5. a   6. b   7. c   8. a   9. d   10. b

Exercise 90 ◆ Selecting Synonyms, p. 145

1. c   2. c   3. a   4. c   5. a   6. b   7. c   8. a   9. b   10. b

Exercise 91 ◆ Review, pp. 146–47

1. b   3. b   5. c   7. a   9. c   11. c   13. b   15. c   17. a   19. b
2. c   4. a   6. a   8. c   10. b   12. c   14. c   16. b   18. b   20. a

Exercise 92 ◆ Suffixes and Prefixes, pp. 147–48

1. a   2. a   3. b   4. c   5. b   6. c   7. c   8. a

Exercise 93 ◆ Spelling Review, pp. 148–49

1. beneficiary
2. cartographer
3. meteorologist
4. pediatrician
5. convalescent
6. actuary
7. dental hygienist
8. ambassador
9. veterinary or veterinarian
10. dietitian

Section eleven

Exercise 94 ◆ Speed of Interpretation, p. 153

Column 1:   1, 4, 5, 7, 9, 11, 14, 15, 17, 20, 26, 28, 29, 32, 33, 35, 39

Column 2:   2, 3, 4, 5, 6, 8, 9, 10, 14, 16, 19, 20, 21, 22, 23, 24, 29, 32, 34, 35, 37

Exercise 95 ◆ Speed of Interpretation, p. 154

Column 1:   1, 2, 6, 9, 10, 18, 20, 21, 23, 24, 25, 29, 31, 34, 35, 37, 38, 40

Column 2:   1, 2, 5, 6, 7, 8, 11, 14, 17, 19, 20, 21, 26, 27, 29, 30, 33, 36, 37, 39, 40

Exercise 96 ◆ Getting the Meaning from the Context, pp. 155–56

1. position requiring little or no work and usually paying well
2. unselfish; thoughtful of the welfare of others
3. guessing; opinion formed without enough evidence for proof
4. rights or privileges belonging to no one else
5. devoted to learning; scholarly
6. spelling
7. accustomed; hardened; habituated
8. roundabout; winding; not straightforward
9. landing place; pier
10. gets through to; understands

Exercise 97 ◆ Finding Synonyms, pp. 156–57

1. d 3. b 5. c 7. b 9. b 11. d 13. a 15. a 17. d 19. b 21. d
2. c 4. b 6. a 8. a 10. b 12. c 14. a 16. d 18. c 20. d 22. b

Exercise 98 ◆ Finding Antonyms, p. 157

1. d 3. c 5. d 7. a 9. a 11. a 13. d 15. a 17. c 19. c 21. c
2. c 4. a 6. b 8. b 10. d 12. a 14. a 16. d 18. a 20. d 22. a

Exercise 99 ◆ Choosing the Correct Word, pp. 158–59

1. council	4. course	7. counsel	10. minor	13. minor
2. bouillon	5. miner	8. affect	11. effect	14. affect
3. decease	6. bullion	9. disease	12. coarse	15. decease

Exercise 100 ◆ Choosing the Correct Word, p. 159

1. fry	3. broil, barbecue	5. barbecue	7. simmer
2. parboil	4. bake	6. boil	8. toast

Exercise 101 ◆ Supplying the Correct Word, pp. 159–60

1. bequeath	3. earn	5. contribute	7. subscribe
2. invest	4. lend	6. squander	8. borrow

Exercise 102 ◆ Supplying the Correct Word, p. 160

1. precocious	3. shrewd	5. versatile	7. learned
2. diffident	4. talented	6. wise	8. diligent

Exercise 103 ◆ Supplying the Required Word, pp. 160–61

1. telephone	3. dissent	5. incredulous	7. congregation	9. introspect
2. gregarious	4. monotonous	6. supervision	8. post-mortem	10. sensitivity

Exercise 104 ◆ Review, pp. 161–63

1. c 3. a 5. d 7. d 9. a 11. b 13. d 15. d 17. d 19. d
2. d 4. b 6. a 8. a 10. a 12. b 14. c 16. d 18. b 20. c

Section twelve

Part A ◆ Vocations and Industries, p. 165

1. a   2. c   3. b   4. c   5. a   6. b   7. b   8. b   9. a   10. c

Part B ◆ Specialists, p. 166

1. b   2. c   3. a   4. c   5. a   6. c   7. a   8. c   9. c   10. c

Part C ◆ Nouns from Tomorrow's Jobs, p. 167

1. b   2. a   3. b   4. a   5. b   6. a   7. c   8. a   9. a   10. c

Part D ◆ Words Often Confused, p. 168

1. principle
2. veracity
3. stationery
4. prescribe
5. principal
6. proscribe
7. counsel
8. affect
9. complement
10. emigrant

Part E ◆ Getting the Meaning from the Context, pp. 168–70

1. long life
2. tendency to say little
3. implied or understood without being openly expressed
4. movable; easily moved
5. concise
6. at the same time; together
7. stinginess; extreme economy
8. forewarnings
9. accidental; happening by chance
10. unselfish person; one concerned with the welfare of others
11. of motion
12. noisy, loud-mouthed, or showy
13. secret, concealed
14. irritable; easily made angry
15. enduring; lasting a long time; lasting through the years
16. rapid and repeated production
17. using too many words for the same idea
18. misgivings; doubts
19. checked; restrained
20. enunciating; putting into words

Part F ◆ Analogies, pp. 171–73

1. a:c or c:a
2. e:c
3. e:a
4. d:e or e:d
5. e:c
6. d:c
7. a:c or c:a
8. c:b
9. e:b
10. e:a
11. d:c
12. a:b or b:a
13. e:d
14. a:d
15. c:b
16. c:a
17. a:e
18. e:b
19. b:c
20. b:e
21. d:e or e:d
22. a:d or d:a
23. c:e
24. e:c
25. d:c

Part G ◆ Word Parts, pp. 173–74

1. all
2. after
3. earth
4. distant
5. self
6. between
7. under
8. back, again, back again
9. time
10. well
11. beforehand
12. one
13. not
14. make, cause to be
15. not
16. across, over
17. against
18. state of, condition of
19. without
20. make, cause to be
21. carry
22. place for
23. turn
24. not, away from
25. around

Part H ◆ Listing Synonyms and Antonyms, p. 174

1. Any 5: adept, adroit, deft, clever, apt, proficient, dexterous
2. Any 5: accept, receive, get, steal, pocket, gather, snatch, abduct
3. Any 5: ancient, venerable, antique, archaic, obsolete, aged
4. Any 5: benign, generous, good, humane, forbearing, obliging, friendly
5. Any 5: big, huge, enormous, significant, great, large, massive, vast, immense

Part I ◆ Spelling, p. 175

1. liquefy
2. acquittal
3. occurrence
4. parallel
5. embarrass
6. gauge
7. amateur
8. weird
9. prophesy
10. propeller

Part J ◆ Meanings of General Words, pp. 175–80

1. d	6. a	11. b	16. b	21. c	26. a	31. d	36. a	41. b	46. c
2. b	7. c	12. d	17. a	22. a	27. a	32. c	37. a	42. a	47. b
3. a	8. b	13. a	18. c	23. d	28. c	33. d	38. b	43. d	48. c
4. b	9. a	14. c	19. c	24. b	29. b	34. a	39. c	44. d	49. d
5. a	10. b	15. b	20. a	25. a	30. b	35. b	40. d	45. d	50. a